Myself
& Some
Other
Being

T0108608

ROBERT D. RICHARDSON

series editor

Myself & Some Other Being

Wordsworth and the Life Writing

DANIEL ROBINSON

UNIVERSITY OF IOWA PRESS

IOWA CITY

University of Iowa Press, Iowa City 52242
Copyright © 2014 by Daniel Robinson
www.uiowapress.org
Printed in the United States of America

Design by Richard Hendel

The University of Iowa Press is a member
of Green Press Initiative and is committed
to preserving natural resources.

Printed on acid-free paper

Library of Congress
Cataloguing-in-Publication Data
Robinson, Daniel.
Myself and some other being: Wordsworth and
the life writing / by Daniel Robinson.
pages cm. — (Muse books)
Includes bibliographical references and index.
ISBNS: 978-1-60938-232-2, 1-60938-232-3 (pbk.)
ISBNS: 978-1-60938-258-2, 1-60938-258-7 (ebk)
1. Wordsworth, William, 1770–1850. Prelude.
2. Autobiographical poetry, English. I. Title.
PR5864.R63 3014
821'.7 — dc23   2013037838

Holding onto myself by the hand,
I change places into the spirit
I had as a rack-ribbed child,
And walk slowly out through my mind
To the wood, as into a falling fire. . . .
—JAMES DICKEY

We turn back, always bowing to that urge
To return, to revise, to be certain. What do we want?
Everything we can never get.
—DAN ALBERGOTTI

contents

Note on Editions

For ease of reference, I cite the 2010 paperback selection of Wordsworth's poems edited by Stephen Gill. Unless otherwise indicated, all citations of Wordsworth's poetry and prose refer to this edition: *William Wordsworth* (21st-Century Oxford Authors), edited by Stephen Gill (Oxford: Oxford UP, 2010), which includes the thirteen-book version of *The Prelude*, the version to which I most often refer. When I cite line numbers for poetry, I also provide page numbers in parentheses.

Keeping the different versions of *The Prelude* straight is difficult, especially since Wordsworth did not entitle any of them "The Prelude." In addition to the published version of 1850, three complete versions exist in manuscript. They are all *The Prelude*. Since doubt lingers over the authoritative status of the posthumously published text, scholars in recent decades have taken advantage of being able to read and study the three manuscript versions that, presumably, better reflect the author's intentions for the work at three different stages. The first version is untitled but exists in two parts identified as such by Wordsworth. This short draft is known as the two-part *Prelude* of 1798–1799 and is often treated as a complete work, although it may be only an aborted attempt at a longer work. Three years later, Wordsworth began expanding the poem; the thirteen-book *Prelude*, as it is known, was completed in 1805 and was preserved in fair copies made in 1805–1806. First published in 1926, this version has a working title, "Poem Title not yet fixed upon by William Wordsworth Addressed to S. T. Coleridge," and is the preferred version because it was written during what experts have called "the Great Decade," 1798–1807, when Wordsworth wrote all of the poems that have been the most popular since early in the twentieth century. Some critics maintain, however, that the fourteen-book *Prelude*, published in 1850, is an improved poem. All three are available in the Norton Critical Edition, *The Prelude: 1799, 1805, 1850*, ed. Jonathan Wordsworth, M. H. Abrams, and Stephen Gill (Norton, 1979). Extensive details and a full critical apparatus for each version may be found in the Cornell Wordsworth edition: *The Prelude, 1798–1799*, ed. by Stephen Parrish (Cornell University Press, 1977); *The Thirteen-Book Prelude*, 2 vols., ed. by Mark L. Reed (Cornell University Press, 1991); and *The Fourteen-Book Prelude*, ed. by W. J. B. Owen (Cornell University Press, 1985).

Myself
& Some
Other
Being

Prelude

We Poets in our youth begin in gladness;
But thereof comes in the end despondency and madness.[1]

Nearing the completion of the thirteen-book draft of his autobiographical poem *The Prelude*, William Wordsworth wrote to his friend Sir George Beaumont in 1805 that it is "a thing unprecedented in Literary history that a man should talk so much about himself." He adds that doing so "is not self-conceit . . . but real humility," having begun the poem "because I was unprepared to treat any more arduous subject and diffident of my own powers."[2] Having settled on nearly 8500 lines of iambic pentameter for the story of his life, Wordsworth thought he had finished the project he began in the fall of 1798. The poem, however, would remain unread by anyone other than a handful of Wordsworth's closest friends and family for close to half a century. Wordsworth would edit, rewrite, delete, add, and otherwise tinker with those lines during most of that time.

Over the decades of revision the poem's original chronology, a span that focuses on Wordsworth's earliest memories and most formative experiences leading up to the 1798 *Lyrical Ballads*, his collaboration with Samuel Taylor Coleridge, is maintained. These years are the "determined bounds" of his poem, and those demarcations never change.[3] Living until the age of 80, Wordsworth had many more years to add to the poem about his life, but he never did. *The Prelude*, then, is the prelude to a career, a writing life that begins with *Lyrical Ballads*. In *The Prelude*, which he would describe as the "history of a poet's mind," Wordsworth finds that the source of his creativity is in what already has happened and discovers that the instrument of his creativity is writing, talking "so much," about himself.

1

The Prelude; or Growth of a Poet's Mind, an Autobiographical Poem is the full title given to the poem by Wordsworth's executors for publication in 1850, just a few weeks after the poet's death. Not a conventional autobiography by any means, *The Prelude* is life writing of a peculiar kind — epic memoir in blank verse.[4] In this letter to Beaumont, Wordsworth admits the uncomfortable self-consciousness of drawing upon personal experience — and the vanity of not only drawing upon personal experience but also treating it as though it were a proper subject for poetry. The poet's remark also signals another concern — the desire to see one's writing as contributing in some significant way to "literature," as staking a claim for oneself in "literary history." *The Prelude*, then, is about finding one's place among other writers, the living and the dead. But that after-life is reserved for the writer, not the real person. Ironically, Wordsworth presumed that literary immortality would come as the result of other work, not *The Prelude*. He had to write those 8500 lines because he had to first exist before he could live forever.

Wordsworth writes *The Prelude* to write that self into existence. This person, the life writing (that is, the living person doing the writing), William Wordsworth, writes his life in the hope of finding words worthy of writing himself as a writer, as *Wordsworth*. Those two words, "words" and "worth," are essential, in more ways than one, to Wordsworth's identity. After all, this was a precocious teenager who signed his first published poem with the pseudonym *Axiologus* — a transliterated pun in Greek that means "the worth of words," or "words' worth."

The Wordsworth who is the subject of *Myself and Some Other Being* is just a few years older, in his late 20s and early 30s. He believes he is destined to be a writer but has to figure out what kind of writer he is supposed to be. More important, he must convince himself that what he has to say is necessary. So, he writes about his life in order to justify his writing life — chiefly to himself. The heart of this book focuses on writing Wordsworth did in Germany, during a miserable winter that made him appreciate memories of home and that made him re-envision himself in relation to those memories. Soon after finishing *Lyrical Ballads*, he began writing the fragments that would become *The Prelude* as well as other poems that are significant to the subject of memory and life-writing. This book is roughly chronological, following Wordsworth from when he begins his career in earnest through the completion of the first major draft of *The Prelude*, in which he confirms his calling. I want to catch Wordsworth in the progress of becoming *Wordsworth* — not by writing his life so much as by reading his life-writing.

The Prelude is Wordsworth's "portrait of the artist as a young man." So are the several smaller poems that I will address; they are miniatures. Wordsworth has what I like to call a memorial imagination: I want to show how Wordsworth's writing explores memory in cooperation with imagination as a means to understand the life writing as part of beginning the writing life. This exploration involves the making, literally the *poetics*, of past, present, and future as a fiction of identity and, in the case of autobiographical writing, of identity as authority. It is a fiction, not because it is factitious, but because whether it is or is not is unimportant. What matters is the making. Memory, the fiction of lived experience, of a remembered/imagined past, is creative and therefore is no less true — is perhaps more true, when a writer fashions it into form. This is a point upon which Blake would argue with Wordsworth: in the margins of his copy of the latter's 1815 *Poems*, Blake writes bluntly, "Imagination has nothing to do with Memory."[5] To Wordsworth, memory is just a different form of imagination, another kind of making — one that only appears to be based on a true story. In this way, all life-writing is like adaptation, the appropriation of source material — one's life, the originary text — for expression in a different medium.

As an adaptation of the poet's memory, *The Prelude* is about how memory negotiates the past, making the past into something relevant to the present—a present that involves the real presence of people and influences that color the way one reflects on one's past. Wordsworth is concerned with the same questions all writers ask: How can I express the subjective experience of my life in a way that matters to others? How can I keep myself out of my writing? Should I even try? Perhaps more so than any writer before him, Wordsworth examines what it means to write about oneself, to draw upon memories, and to transform those memories into something that may be valuable for other people to read.

Wordsworth also wants to interpret this writerly self to Coleridge, the addressee of *The Prelude*, who is also Wordsworth's friend, fan, mentor, taskmaster, critic, and albatross. (Wordsworth and Coleridge are the Lennon and McCartney of English literature.) Coleridge is the poem's ideal reader; and the Wordsworth that Wordsworth writes is, therefore, at least partly Wordsworth's estimation of the Wordsworth that Coleridge would want to read. In an early draft, Wordsworth explains to Coleridge that he has written it "To understand myself" and to provide his confederate and confidant "With better knowledge how the heart was framed / Of him thou lovest."[6] So, this intensely personal yet highly literary mediation of self and memory, present and past has always been meant for another writer to read. In this light, *The Prelude* is a memorial of their collaboration and their friendship—a friendship that became irreparably fractured, though partly restored in later years. Wordsworth wrote the poem for Coleridge in the enthusiasm of their shared ideals and ambitions. But Wordsworth's poem for his friend also emerged out of loneliness, isolation, anxiety, doubt, insecurity. Like all writing.

Wordsworth is known for some familiar catchphrases that have become shibboleths of creative writing—"language

really used by men," "the spontaneous overflow of powerful feeling," "emotion recollected in tranquility," "a poet is a
man speaking to men," and so on.[7] As writers, we sometimes
think writing *should* be merely "the spontaneous overflow of
powerful feeling" — that is, a kind of writing out of the moment, an effusion. But this is not really what Wordsworth
means. In 1800 "the spontaneous overflow of powerful feeling," meant deliberately to summon the feeling apposite to
the subject. We tend to forget that Wordsworth means that
the poet conjures these feelings during the "emotion recollected in tranquility" part of the process.

But nobody needs me to enucleate nuggets of wisdom
from the preface to *Lyrical Ballads*. Most of the time, writers
don't understand what they're doing anyway. William
Blake, for example, couldn't believe that Wordsworth actually wrote the several essays he published in his 1815 *Poems*.
Blake scrawled in the margins, "I do not know who wrote
these Prefaces[;] they are very mischievous & direct[sic]
contrary to Wordsworths[sic] own Practise[sic]."[8] In those
would-be manifestoes, Wordsworth is too defensive to be of
much help to aspiring writers. But knowing that he was so
defensive and so anxious makes Wordsworth the emergent
writer a more congenial figure than does what he says about
writing poetry, which, as Blake suggests, might seem at odds
with the poetry he wrote.

Therefore, I ask that you forget the stodgy-seeming
Wordsworth you may remember from your Brit-lit survey
and imagine instead a young writer, both ambitious and in-
secure, who is cognizant of his potential and his originality
but is uncertain about whether or not anyone will buy what
he's selling. Indeed, for many years, few did buy it. But just
enough of the public read Wordsworth to threaten the status
quo and thus to incur scorn and ridicule from the pens of
critics and fellow poets. "This will never do" is the exasper-
ated and memorable opening to Francis Jeffrey's damning
review of Wordsworth's long poem *The Excursion* in 1814.[9]

This long, didactic, and generally tedious poem in nine books was intended to be only part of the magnum opus Wordsworth hoped to write. Keats thought it was one of the "things to rejoice at in this Age," but *The Excursion* proved to be a poem only the Victorians could love.[10] Seven years later, in *Don Juan*, Lord Byron is still harping on Wordsworth's "drowsy frowzy poem, call'd the 'Excursion' / Writ in a manner which is my aversion."[11] Gradually, *The Excursion* was recognized as a great work (and then dropped out of favor again in the twentieth century). From the start, however, Wordsworth worried a lot about his career, about being misunderstood, and about making enough money to keep writing. Years before *The Excursion* "dropped stillborn from the press," such concerns recalled to Wordsworth the fates of Thomas Chatterton and Robert Burns, two poets who died young and penniless: "We Poets in our youth begin in gladness; / But thereof comes in the end despondency and madness."[12] So, to ward off this end, by writing *The Prelude*, the young Wordsworth gropes for the known past in the face of a discouraging present and an unknowable future. It wasn't all daffodils.

The direction of *The Prelude*—as its title signifies—is forward, not backward, even though it is ostensibly about the past. But even the future anticipated in the poem is the creative work of the imaginative moment. In the "story-world" of the poem, Wordsworth's writing is happening now, just as readers' experiences of the poem happen in that same moment. Therefore, the writer, the immortal one, is right there with you. If there's one thing that Wordsworth's poetry shows, it's that the writing of one's *life* may sustain the life writing it by giving a sense of purpose, of being, of belonging—and of becoming. Of "something evermore about to be."[13]

Two Consciousnesses

A tranquillizing spirit presses now
On my corporeal frame: so wide appears
The vacancy between me and those days,
Which yet have such self-presence in my mind
That, sometimes, when I think of them, I seem
Two consciousnesses, conscious of myself
And of some other Being.[1]

In these lines from *The Prelude*, Wordsworth explains the relationship between the remembered past and the active, creative present — that is, the life writing — as his experience of seeming to be "two consciousnesses": "Myself," he writes, and "some other Being." This "being" is basically a now-self seeking to define itself in relation to a then-self that does not really exist (perhaps never did). When he thinks back on his former self, he is struck by the distance between himself now and what he thinks is his past. The "I" here consists of a double consciousness only one that is identifiable as "myself." The "other Being" is part memory, which, for Wordsworth, necessarily involves invention. The writing of *The Prelude* begins in the discovery of the "two consciousnesses" of "Tintern Abbey" — the remembered (and, therefore, partly imagined) past self and the present self writing that past self onto paper, fixing it into form. Writing *The Prelude* Wordsworth more fully explores his sense of himself and of his past self as "some other Being."

The most original aspect of *The Prelude* is that the model of the epic and its traditional modes of adaptation and transmutation provide Wordsworth with a way of thinking about his own history and about how, as a writer, he is free to adapt his personal history and his poetic identity to suit his creative needs through the very act of writing. In effect, he becomes both the hero and the bard of his own epic, an odyssey of his own mind. But as a self-conscious literary performance, *The Prelude* is not so much a rumination on Wordsworth's actual past as it is a poetics of memoir, a construction of memories, and a process of memorializing oneself and transforming the past into something that only exists now for a reader. The past does not exist: it is a fiction, it is cognitive material that the creative imagination may forge into something that does exist — the memoir, the lyric, the thinly-veiled autobiographical fiction, or even the personal epic.

As an autobiographical epic (a pretty audacious enterprise), *The Prelude* is a poem about what it means to write the self, to imagine a version of one's life that is not strictly autobiographical but that serves other — one might even say, higher — literary purposes than confession or memoir. That is to say, Wordsworth's poem is a narrative about the adaptation of memories of one's past for the purposes of the writing moment in process, which is itself an activity of self-engendering and a fiction of authority that is meant to appear to the reader as if it is happening in concert with the reading of it.

But the poem is also meant to be read and to be understood. And to be useful. After Wilde and then the Modernists, taking their cue from Keats's resistance to "poetry that has a palpable design upon us," we are today uncomfortable, disdainful even, of poetry that has the whiff of a didactic purpose.[2] "Every great Poet is a Teacher," Wordsworth insisted, "I wish either to be considered as a Teacher, or as nothing."[3] But he is not interested in teaching you how to be a poet — you have to figure that out for yourself. Instead, he wants to teach you how to have a poetic experience of life, how to *make* memories, not necessarily positive ones but darker ones too, into an ever-present source of spiritual — and moral — restoration. Wordsworth wants to show you how to *make*, to make memories, to make your life into story—to, in the words of Morrissey, sing your life. Wordsworth believed that his own practice has refined his imagination so that he can describe how the creative process of life works on him and how he can use it. Wordsworth's life writing about his writing life shows that being creative means you never actually *become* creative, as if that were the endpoint. You are always *being* creative and you never finish—even when you fail to produce—as long as your mind is doing something.

The template for Wordsworth's peculiar brand of life writing is "Lines Written a Few Miles above Tintern Abbey on Revisiting the Banks of the Wye during a Tour, July 13, 1798" which we shorthand as "Tintern Abbey," even though Wordsworth never mentions that ruin in the poem. The reference in the title is more a place marker to locate Wordsworth at a particular spot where he stood five years prior to the now of the poem. This poem demonstrates that, for Wordsworth, writing about one's past involves one's imagination as much as it does—possibly even more than—one's memories; memory and imagination are bound up together in a mutually generative process. Wordsworth recognizes a past self that once considered itself a present self, while the current present self can only imagine that past. "Tintern Abbey" provides the motto for Wordsworth's autobiographical enterprise: "I cannot paint / What then I was."[4] But then he tries to do it anyway, even if it is impossible.

Like *The Prelude*, "Tintern Abbey" is also about the present and the future. The poem commemorates Wordsworth's revisiting the place with his sister, Dorothy, who is seeing it for the first time. They had reunited a few years earlier, having lived many years apart with different relatives after the deaths of their parents. Although her presence is not revealed until the end of the poem, we learn that Wordsworth's experience of visiting this place is better because he is there with his sister, who he hopes will have the same renovating memories of the place that he has had. And these memories will only get better themselves in the future. Wordsworth thus bids a not-so-fond farewell to his twenties; he is grateful to be the person he is now, asserting that along with the loss of his younger adult self comes the loss of certain responses he no longer wishes to feel, those "aching joys" and those "dizzy raptures."[5] In Wordsworth's poetry, memory involves loss because the mind cannot re-create an experience; it can only make a memory that is more or less accurate.

Now, five years later, Wordsworth asserts that his original experience of nature has provided him the imaginative, moral, and spiritual sustenance necessary for being fully human. But this happens through the activity of memory, so memory is thus active and happening now. Nature, green nature with a capital-N, is important to Wordsworth not only because it is lovely but also because its loveliness has a profoundly benevolent effect on the mind and the heart. The mechanisms for this salutary effect are memory and imagination, often indistinguishable from one another. In exchange for what he has lost, the previous experience, Wordsworth asserts what he calls "Abundant recompence." His present self is more compassionate now that he can hear the "still, sad music of humanity"; moreover, he has gained "a sense sublime" that gives him a spiritual awareness of the underlying unity of all things.[6] These abilities are essential to his calling because, though Wordsworth is often thought of as a nature poet, he is most interested in how he can translate the benevolent moral influence nature has had on him into poetry that can do the same for us. Everyone, Wordsworth would argue, can do this, but not everyone does or even knows how to make memory work in this way. What makes the poet necessary is that he can teach you how to do this by modeling it for you.

Wordsworth is interested in the specialized coordination between imagination and memory in the mind of a poet and the benevolent influence that coordination has on the "moral being" of the poet and of the reader.[7] To understand this, you must keep in mind that Wordsworth grants that even perception itself is creative: he celebrates the development in himself of his love for "all the mighty world / Of eye and ear, both what they half create, / And what perceive."[8] For Wordsworth, all experience comprises half perception and half creation. It is an epistemology halfway between Lockean empiricism and Blakean mysticism. Blake writes, "as a man is, so he sees"; Locke might have written, "as a man sees, so he is."[9] For Wordsworth, perception is not only an epistemological object of inquiry but a poetical one as well, in the sense that it is the mind's attempt to understand the relationship between its knowing and its making. This is why it is important that Wordsworth thinks of *The Prelude* as "the history of a Poet's mind," and not merely as the history of William Wordsworth's life to age twenty-eight.

Memory and imagination, knowledge and creativity. There's an equation in there somewhere, but working it out may not matter because in Wordsworth's work, it's all ultimately ontological. So, for Wordsworth, knowing requires knowing ourselves, but that knowledge comes from having experience with *things* outside of ourselves and making memories within — thereby making ourselves — so that we may impart our knowledge to others through what we make, what we write. Wordsworth explains that he has developed a meditative practice that seems like Zen: in that "serene and blessed mood," activated by memory working with imagination, Wordsworth writes,

> we are laid asleep
> In body, and become a living soul:
> While with an eye made quiet by the power

Of harmony, and the deep power of joy,
We see into the life of things.[10]

The word "things" usually has a bland meaninglessness; few
writers could use it with as much deep resonance as Wordsworth does. Here, he means actual things, as in all things in
the material world — not only inanimate objects but organic
beings too. Here, the visionary power only implicitly, or inci-
dentally, pertains to creativity even as it is closely associated
with memory: this vision derives from the influence — even
subconsciously — of previously seen "forms of beauty" on
the mind when it is "absent long."[11] The visionary power
becomes in *The Prelude* and other later works more essential to literary creativity. Wordsworth believed that poets in
particular develop this vision as a kind of expertise that they
pass on to their readers.

Even in his famous daffodils poem, "I Wandered Lonely
as a Cloud," which we might not take as seriously as we do,
say, "Tintern Abbey," Wordsworth asserts that a poet, already predisposed to process experience more deeply than
most people, is able to quicken spontaneously imaginative reconstructions of previous experiences. I think of this
poem as distinctly meta-poetic. This power is not merely the
ordinary processes of memory; it involves the more extraor-
dinary processes of imagination. The daffodils poem, for instance, concludes with the speaker, who is unmistakably a
poet / the poet, "in vacant or in pensive mood": here, the
sudden image of the previously experienced daffodils acti-
vates a new visual image adapted by the creative mind —
"They flash upon that inward eye."[12] The mind's eye receives
an image from the poet's memory — it is as if the daffodils
bring the image of themselves into being — and the poet is
able to feel the kindred pleasure that he did when he saw
them in person, but it has become one that is an imaginative
advance upon the original. "And then my heart with plea-

sure fills," he writes, "And dances with the Daffodils."[13] The poem is simple and seems a bit hokey to us today; but for Wordsworth, dancing with the daffodils is serious business. The process he describes in both this poem and "Tintern Abbey" is sophisticated, and the power to re-view is essential in the most philosophical sense of the word. The poetic inscribed there says much about the writing of one's self and the adaptation of experience to poetry. An English professor I know (me) inculcates an important lesson to his students: "It's not about the fucking daffodils!"

But I hope this remark, gleefully preserved in more than a few undergraduates' notebooks, is not just flippant vulgarity. The daffodils are objects subordinate to the poet's mind, which is the actual subject of the poem. Yet, as Wordsworth asserts, we can go back to the same place (or poem) but we can never have the same experience because we are not the same. The place (or poem) may not change but we do. In this way memory always involves loss—because the past becomes, in effect, imaginary, nonmaterial inventory. So does one's former self.

Wordsworth is often thought of as a "nature" poet— probably because of the daffodils. But he more accurately might be thought of as a "life" or as a "things" poet—not simply because he writes about his life, but because he is interested in *things* that are alive. In what is now known as the "Christabel Notebook" because it contains the earliest surviving lines from Coleridge's poem "Christabel," Wordsworth began sketching out some philosophical ideas—in blank verse—on life and things, which ended up in greatly revised (but not improved) form in Book Nine of *The Excursion*:

> There is an active principle alive in all things:
> In all things, in all natures, in the flowers
> And in the trees, in every pebbly stone

> That paves the brooks, the stationary rocks
> The moving waters, and the invisible air.
> All beings have their properties which spread
> Beyond themselves, a power by which they make
> Some other being conscious of their life. . . .[14]

"Things" and "beings" are frequently synonymous in Wordsworth, for they represent the same entity but often, as in the lines above, there is an implied spiritual development from the state of "thing-ness" to the state of "being-ness"—as Wordsworth's process of thought itself uncovers the "underpresence" (a word he uses later) in the "life of things." The "power" of which Wordsworth speaks is imaginative, creative, so he is being rightly figurative. But this is not what John Ruskin would call the "pathetic fallacy," by which a writer portrays inanimate objects as if they had human feelings; nor is it exactly Immanuel Kant's unknowable *Ding an sich*, ("thing per se"), or the barely knowable noumenon. Like the noumenon, and thus unlike the phenomenon, this "being-ness" is not known by the senses; in Wordsworth this "active principle" is recognized by the imagination but without imputing to the thing human qualities. It is more the other way around—we, in perceiving it, are becoming more like the thing *qua* being. So, in another sense, the "there is" assertion is the act of the writing; that act brings these things to life, giving them being as ideas—not just words.

Like "things," "being" is another Wordsworthian keyword. He alternates between "being" as a noun signifying static existence and "being" as a gerund replete with implied action—as in the remarkable phrase describing our first years of life as "the years of unrememberable being."[15] Or as in his sense of himself and of his past self as "some other Being," a phrase he also uses in the passage above from the "Christabel Notebook." In "Tintern Abbey," he writes that he recognizes

In nature and the language of the sense,
The anchor of my purest thoughts, the nurse,
The guide, the guardian of my heart, and soul
Of all my moral being.[16]

Here, Wordsworth is not saying that he is a "moral being" or
even that he has become a "moral being" but that he has a
"moral being." And certainly he means for us to understand
that that "being" is not fixed or static. In Wordsworth, the
noun "being," as in the phrase "creature that exists," plays
subtly with or against the gerundive sense of "being" as a
noun synonymous with "existence" — does not existence
necessarily imply something that is *existing*? Therefore
"being" always involves the participle "becoming." Both
eventually imply "was" — whether we like it or not. But in
poetry "being" may be "limitless." Then, may not infinite
being be also a process of "becoming"? The *Oxford Dictionary of English* does define to "become" as to "begin to be."
Try to put that in the past tense. It's like having to think in
terms of an infinitive verb "to was."

Wordsworth began writing the fragments that would become *The Prelude* just a few months after writing "Tintern
Abbey" in July of 1798. Within the next year, he completed
two parts of around 500 lines each that cover his early childhood and schooldays. Wordsworth discovers — or invents —
in these years, his earliest experiences, what he claims to
have gained by the time he writes "Tintern Abbey." It is as
if writing *The Prelude* makes Wordsworth worry that he has
lost more than he has gained. So, he returned to it again and
again mostly because he was revisiting himself years later,
just as he revisited that spot near Tintern Abbey. He wanted
to review his progress.

Because of this revisiting of the text, *The Prelude* exists in
many different stages and in various degrees of complete-
ness. None of them is more authoritative than another because Wordsworth never published a clearly definitive text.

In each version what Wordsworth describes as "two consciousnesses" are necessarily altered by time, by being and becoming—as in "Tintern Abbey." For writers especially, the "two consciousnesses" are at work—hopefully in collaboration or at least cooperation—in every representation of self. It doesn't really matter, as it were, whether it is fictional or non-fictional autobiography; the creative work is similar. James Dickey, who, with the possible exception of Seamus Heaney, may be the most Wordsworth-like poet since Wallace Stevens, speaks in terms similar to Wordsworth's "some other Being," and what it means for poetry. Dickey describes a "poetic agent" who acts as the Wordsworthian "man speaking to men" via the representational "I-figure," otherwise known as the speaker who is in possession of the past experiences described in a poem. As Dickey writes in *Sorties*,

> The I-figure does not live in the real world of fact but in a kind of magical abstraction, an emotion- and thought-charged personal version of it. Rather than in a place where objects and people have the taciturn and indisputable tangibility, the stolid solidity, of fact, the poetic agent inhabits a realm more rich and strange and a good deal "thicker" than reality, for it gathers to itself all the analogies and associations—either obvious or far-fetched—that the poetic mind as it ranges through the time and space of its existence can bring to the subject.[17]

Both the "poetic agent" and the "I-figure" are avatars, *versionings* of the self. Wordsworth and Dickey emphasize the poet's ability to handle "absent things as if they were present." This is an oblique description of memory working in tandem with the imagination.

"Things" do not usually absent themselves; but they do in Wordsworth because he wants to emphasize the power of memory to present, to make present, to *re-present* things that had been "absent." In the preface to *Lyrical Ballads*, Wordsworth writes that the poet has

> an ability of conjuring up in himself passions, which are indeed far from being the same as those produced by real events, yet (especially in those parts of the general sympathy which are pleasing and delightful) do more nearly resemble the passions produced by real events, than any thing which, from the motions of their own minds merely, other men are accustomed to feel in themselves; whence, and from practice, he has acquired a greater readiness and power in expressing what he thinks and feels, and especially those thoughts and feelings which, by his own choice, or from the structure of his own mind, arise in him without immediate external excitement.[18]

Conjuring is a kind of making. Dickey and Wordsworth are saying the same thing: even when the poet is writing about himself and his past experiences, he is nonetheless creating not a divided but a double self: one, the subject, who is a representative of common humanity even as the other, the poet giving words to that subject, partakes of something richer, from some other place. For Wordsworth, the creative activity is more intense when writing the self because of the effort required to believe that one's self, if not coherent, is at least contiguous.

Writing these poems about memory and imagination, about "myself and some other being," has made Wordsworth acutely aware that everything he writes is a versioning of the self. And so it never stops — there always will be "two consciousnesses," maybe more. This is probably true of everything any writer writes; but the process of autobiographical writing requires both a delimiting of what may constitute the work and an engendering of a textual self that exists only in the autobiographical work. In *The Prelude*, he confesses to Coleridge (the addressee of the poem) that he fears he has begun the story of his life too early out of, as he writes, "The weakness of a human love for days / Disowned by memory."[19] The chief theme of this 1799 poem is the formative influence of nature on the young boy's imagination. And, as the phrase "disowned by memory" implies, much of what Wordsworth recalls is actually constitutive speculation. The "weakness," then, is the "human love" for, or tendency toward, the fantasy of formation in place of actual memories, the desire to write a fiction of one's self to fill in the gaps and to make coherent the fragments of existence.

By the time he writes "Tintern Abbey," Wordsworth knows he wants to be a writer. But before he can really figure out what kind of writer he wants to be, he needs to be sure that this desire to write has some legitimate justification within himself. He can't just want to be a writer; he tries to find evidence in himself that he is supposed to be a writer. He looks for it in his memory, and in the course of this inner seeking comes to begin making himself. Wordsworth finds this justification, his poetic calling, if you will, in his experience of nature. But the revelation of one's calling doesn't have to be the same as Wordsworth climbing Mount Snowdon; it could be listening to Roy Orbison records, or flying night missions over Japan during World War II. Or, simply, it could be seeing the sublime in the mundane — a mark on the wall or a world in a grain of sand.[20]

Four years later, writing the first stanzas of what would become "Intimations of Immortality," Wordsworth is no longer quite so confident in the abundance of the recompense — or even in how compensatory his lately gained perspective is. In the "Intimations" ode, which Emerson called "the high-water mark which the intellect has reached in this age," Wordsworth laments that "The things which I have seen I now can see no more."[21] It is all a matter of perception: when he writes that "there hath passed away a glory from the earth," he knows that the glory is not really gone; rather, he cannot see it anymore.[22] He fears he has exhausted his creativity or somehow squandered that gift. The enigmatic "thoughts that do often lie too deep for tears" that Wordsworth appreciates at the end of the ode may be nothing more than a powerful gratitude for the version of the self that the poem has created. In "Tintern Abbey" Wordsworth actually says nothing about his pre-adult self; the past self in that poem existed only five years ago. The difference is that he has begun writing *The Prelude*; so the memory of that pre-adult self is practically all that matters—"O joy! that in our embers / Is something that doth live."[23] Embers are both residual and reproductive; thus we put the present in relation to the past and to the future. We are never really on fire—we only think we were or still hope to be.

The History of a Poet's Mind

When thou dost to that summer turn thy thoughts,
And hast before thee all which then we were,
To thee, in memory of that happiness
It will be known, by thee at least, my Friend,
Felt, that the history of a Poet's mind
Is labour not unworthy of regard.
To thee the work shall justify itself.[1]

Near his thirty-first birthday in 1801, Wordsworth claimed that his life had been "unusually barren of events."[2] He was lying. Perhaps even to himself. The last decade of the eighteenth century had been particularly eventful, often deeply distressing, and profoundly formative for the poet. After surviving the 1790s, Wordsworth at first sought to disavow, to supplant, to forget, the experiences of his twenties. In December of 1799, he settled with his sister, Dorothy, at Dove Cottage near Grasmere, Cumberland, among his beloved lakes, rills, cataracts, and crags, not far from the villages where he had been born and raised. The bulk of *The Prelude*, begun earlier that year in Goslar (as we shall see in the next chapter), is devoted to figuring out who he had been in relation to the man he had become by 1798, and as a way of understanding the writer he thought he would continue to become over the next five decades. With the publication of *Lyrical Ballads* in 1798 came the promise of a literary career; and with the end of the century came the promise of the start of a new life.

Wordsworth addresses *The Prelude* to Coleridge because they were together during the summer of 1798 and were finishing work on *Lyrical Ballads*. "[I]n memory of that happiness," Wordsworth hopes, Coleridge will know and, more important, will *feel* "that the history of a Poet's mind / Is labour not unworthy of regard." Wordsworth's addresses to Coleridge echo Augustine's refrain in the *Confessions* "I write this book for love of your love" — except that Augustine is talking to God.[3] Wordsworth seeks a similar approbation from Coleridge, having himself had something like a conversion that enables him to know that "other Being" he was becoming. He has learned that composition — his preferred term for "writing" — is conversion in the act, happening again, over and over. It is renewed life — again and always.

Coleridge knew Wordsworth was a gifted poet before Wordsworth did. To Coleridge he was "the Giant Wordsworth" and was destined to write a great work "to benefit mankind."[4] As early as 1796, before Wordsworth had written any of his best-known poems, Coleridge declared Wordsworth "the best poet of the age" — a view shared by no one for years to come.[5] Sharing similar literary aspirations, each read the other's work with mutual admiration. Coleridge determined Wordsworth's tragedy *The Borderers* (seldom read today) to be on par with any by Shakespeare. One great bard thus matched, Coleridge encouraged (no doubt hectored) Wordsworth to write the great epic to rival Milton's *Paradise Lost*. A similar ambition had driven Milton, Dante, and Virgil. The ambition of writing an epic as good as Milton's was not unlike the cliché of any writer aspiring to write the Great American Novel. Before Wordsworth, many now-unknown poets had attempted to do battle with Milton in the epic arena. Milton trounced them all. Eventually, poets gave up trying.

For Wordsworth and Coleridge, Milton was still the man to beat. And it was not long before the two contrived a challenge. It was not *The Prelude*, which has the anomalous status of being the prelude to a work — a poet's *magnum opus* — that does not exist. That great project, Wordsworth's epic throwdown, was to be called "The Recluse," and it was born at the same time Wordsworth and Coleridge developed the concept for *Lyrical Ballads*, back in 1798. It was reading "The

Ruined Cottage," begun in 1797, that showed Coleridge the scope of Wordsworth's potential. Intoxicated by Coleridge's faith in him, Wordsworth wrote excitedly, "I know not anything which will not come within the scope of my plan."[6] The plan, however, was not his but Coleridge's. The original figure of the eponymous rural recluse whose observations of man, nature, and society would renew a culturally, politically, and philosophically dispirited age was originally Coleridge's projection of himself as Wordsworthian.

If *The Prelude* is an epic after all, Coleridge is its perverse muse, even if it was not the epic he envisioned his friend and collaborator creating. When he learned that Wordsworth was writing a poem on his own life instead of the great philosophical epic of the age, Coleridge rebuked, "O let it be the tail-piece of 'The Recluse,' for nothing but 'The Recluse' can I hear patiently."[7] Wordsworth took such a reprimand as a kind of encouragement, for he reciprocally believed Coleridge to be "a great man."[8] His faith in Coleridge's greatness, however, increasingly was tempered by concern for Coleridge's health — mental and physical. Wordsworth expected that Coleridge would at least superintend the composition of "The Recluse" and not just complain about the lack of progress: he writes, "I am very anxious to have your notes for the Recluse. I cannot say how much importance I attach to this[;] if it should please God that I survive you, I should reproach myself for ever in writing the work if I had neglected to procure this help."[9] But this also explains his hope that Coleridge might deem the poem "labour not unworthy of regard" and that to Coleridge, the ideal reader of it, "the work shall justify itself."

For years Coleridge continued to believe "The Recluse" to be forthcoming. "I prophesy immortality to his *Recluse*, as the first & finest philosophical Poem," he decreed in 1804. Praising the image of Wordsworth he had invented, Coleridge writes confidently, "I dare affirm that he will hereafter be admitted as the first & greatest philosophical Poet — the

only man who has effected a compleat and constant synthe-
sis of Thought & Feeling and combined them with Poetic
Forms, with the music of pleasurable passion and with
Imagination."[10] Reserving to himself the role of literary critic
and booster, Coleridge would provide a more balanced as-
sessment of Wordsworth's poetry in the 1817 *Biographia Literaria*, his own innovative experiment in life writing. This
great work finds Coleridge still going on about "The Recluse" with subtle vexation and emphatic admonishment
(in all caps even): "What Mr. Wordsworth *will* produce," he
writes, "it is not for me to prophesy: but I could pronounce
with the liveliest convictions what he is capable of producing. It is the FIRST GENUINE PHILOSOPHIC POEM."[11] If
Wordsworth ever became, strictly speaking, a philosophical
poet, he certainly was not the kind Coleridge envisioned.

The pressure of having to write "The Recluse" according
to Coleridge's specifications drove Wordsworth deeper into
himself and farther away from the plan for "a philosophical
Poem, containing views of Man, Nature, and Society." This
is how he describes his work in the 1814 preface to *The Excursion, Being a Portion of the Recluse, a Poem*. Wordsworth here
makes a public announcement of intent and a promise to
the world that the epic was forthcoming. Wordsworth also
explains the origin of "The Recluse," hinting at *The Prelude*:
"Several years ago," he writes, "when the Author retired to
his native Mountains, with the hope of being enabled to
construct a literary Work that might live, it was a reasonable
thing that he should take a review of his own Mind." This
review resulted, he writes, in an autobiographical "preparatory Poem" that "conducts the history of the Author's mind
to the point when he was emboldened to hope that his facul-
ties were sufficiently matured for entering upon the arduous labour which he had proposed to himself." Wordsworth
locates the origins of *The Prelude*, the "preparatory Poem"
in his own epic ambitions.[12]

The epic that Wordsworth did write turned out to be not

"The Recluse" but *The Prelude*. Without knowing it, Wordsworth gives us an ontological epic — essentially the origin of a writer's creativity. *The Prelude* primarily develops
Wordsworth's recollections/impressions of the first twenty
years of the poet's consciousness. Eliding most of the 1790s,
Wordsworth gives the impression that what were likely his
most exciting and disturbing years, including the five years
between visits to Tintern Abbey, are an irrelevant lacuna.
Wordsworth began writing "the history of a Poet's mind" to
recover the self he had been before the experiences of his
twenties. His youth, adolescence, and select experiences of
young adulthood are the most pertinent to the growth of his
mind, which is really a synecdoche of the life writing about
it. Wordsworth's greatest obligation in *The Prelude* is not to
a chronological narrative of the poet's years, therefore, but
to "the history of a Poet's mind." Reading a new biography
of Wordsworth, therefore, can be irritating when you come
upon verses from *The Prelude* paraphrased as prose, as if the
poem is some kind of reliable source of biographical infor-
mation.

The first version of Wordsworth's poetic history is in two
parts that total only around one thousand lines. This draft,
The Prelude of 1798–99, focuses on the formative years of
childhood and adolescence and concludes at age seventeen,
in 1787, just as the poet is about to go to college. The second part opens with a restatement of what is becoming the
poem's epic argument:

> Thus far my Friend, have we retraced the way
> Through which I travelled when I first began
> To love the woods and fields: the passion yet
> Was in its birth. . . .[13]

This sounds familiar: the two-part *Prelude* is like a more
personal, more specific "Tintern Abbey." When he and his
sister, Dorothy, finally made it home to the vale of Gras-

mere, in December of 1799, Wordsworth saw them as a "pair seceding from the common world" in the hope that, "in the midst of these unhappy times," they might find a "portion of the blessedness which love / And knowledge will, we trust, hereafter give / To all the Vales of earth and all mankind."[14]

The Odyssey in reverse, the longer thirteen- and fourteen-book versions of The Prelude begin with the blissful *nostos* of settling with his sister in the Lake District. By 1799 Wordsworth was writing and editing his life already and could not let the 1799 Prelude rest in peace (or, in two pieces) because he had himself continued to exist. During only six weeks in the spring of 1804 he expanded it to five books; a year later he had another complete version, more fully epic in scope and in allusiveness, now in thirteen books. He tinkered with it for decades, making his final revisions in 1839, when it became fourteen books in order to be more symmetrically epic. But he withheld it from his ever-increasing public because he never felt that he had earned his readers' indulgence. Over several decades, the private writing of The Prelude becomes less private and amorphous as the poem works its way outward from jottings and draftings through numerous and scattered manuscripts to Dorothy Wordsworth, to Coleridge, to his wife and, later, to his daughter, through more extensive revisions, then to other subsidiary readers/helpers/scribes, more editing, and finally to a public reading a dead poet.

But throughout it all the timespan of the poem never changed. In the many surviving versions, the poem always ends in 1798. The life writing the poem would be on display for half a century more. Only after his death did the poem on his life become, ostensibly, The Prelude. At long last Poet Laureate, Wordsworth died on April 23, 1850; The Prelude was in print by July. His widow, Mary, who was, in the words of the poet's nephew, "the best interpreter of his thoughts," gave it the title based on a conception of its relationship to the poet's oeuvre that Wordsworth had outlined in the 1814 preface to *The Excursion*, where he refers to it as a "preparatory Poem" to his poetical works.[15] Mary Wordsworth's title is given in deference to the prophet-poet figure Wordsworth had worked so hard to establish for his public. In other words, from the vantage of the 1850 *Prelude*, the development *The Prelude* delineates is "the prelude" to Wordsworth's becoming that poet. Today we prefer the Wordsworth that some consider to have gone missing a couple of years after completing the thirteen-book *Prelude* in 1805.

So Wordsworth himself never called *The Prelude* "The Prelude." In his preface to *The Excursion*, Wordsworth explains that the "preparatory Poem" on his own life is "addressed to a dear Friend, most distinguished for his knowledge and genius, and to whom the Author's Intellect is deeply indebted."[16] Wordsworth, throughout the decades of revisions to come, preserved his friend's presence in *The Prelude* even as they fell out with each other, tentatively reconciled, and, finally of course, died. Wordsworth disapproved of Coleridge's opium addiction and his uncomfortable-for-everybody fixation on Sara Hutchinson, Wordsworth's wife's sister; Coleridge resented Wordsworth's disapproval and envied his work ethic, if not his success, as well as his harem of adoring females. To understand their dynamic better, you should watch Steve Coogan and Rob Brydon in the 2010 film *The Trip* reenact it with some surprising and hilarious insights that somehow include competing impersonations of Michael Caine.[17]

Despite the dissolution of the friendship, for nearly fifty years the Wordsworth household referred to this poem variously as "the Poem to Coleridge" or "the poem on his/my own life." The title page of the version completed in 1805 reads, in cheeky calligraphy, "Poem Title not yet fixed upon By William Wordsworth Addressed to S. T. Coleridge." By 1819–20 the title had been slightly but significantly altered to read "Poem, Title not fixed upon by William Wordsworth Addressed to his Friend S. T. Coleridge." Jonathan Bate has observed that the dropping of "yet" in the new "Title not fixed upon" suggests that Wordsworth "has given up the idea of ever fixing upon one."[18] Moreover, Wordsworth's apposition of the phrase "his Friend" is poignant, indicating both a touch of regret about the breach with Coleridge and a tinge of pain from a wound that would never heal.

Trances of Thought

Trances of thought and mountings of the mind
Come fast upon me: it is shaken off,
As by miraculous gift 'tis shaken off,
That burthen of my own unnatural self,
The heavy weight of many a weary day
Not mine, and such as were not made for me.[1]

Wordsworth began writing this "history of a poet's mind" addressed to Coleridge during the last year of the eighteenth century, in the coldest winter that century had seen, when he and his sister were far from home, huddled together in a small apartment just within the medieval walls of the German city of Goslar. He was not yet twenty-nine; he had little money, no viable profession, and only the slightest prospect that the book he had deposited at the printers before leaving England the previous autumn might sell. He had also during that summer fallen under the spell of Coleridge's intellect and of that great mind's certainty that Wordsworth was greatest poet living. Or was yet to be. Living up to Coleridge's expectations engendered a crisis of self and of calling in Goslar. Having found sister and mentor, Wordsworth tries to find himself. In the poetic fragments he composed while in Goslar, however, Wordsworth cannot find the then-self to prefigure the self-to-be; he confronts, instead, a now-self lost in "trances of thought" and paralyzed by uncertain being and fearful becoming.

In September of 1798, the collaboration between Wordsworth and Coleridge was still going strong. With *Lyrical Ballads* at press, Wordsworth and his sister travelled to Germany basically so they could bask further in the glow of Coleridge, who, traveling with them, had left his own family behind in England. Desperate for cash, the Wordsworths planned to immerse themselves in the language so they could make money translating German writers into English. But, contrary to expectations, they found it nearly impossible to secure affordable lodgings anywhere near German high culture. Coleridge, by contrast, was travelling on an annuity awarded to him on account of his genius; he was able, therefore, to enjoy sightseeing and socializing. After two weeks with the Wordsworths, irritated by their penury, Coleridge travelled on to Ratzeburg and then to the University of Göttingen, where he was keen to study the latest in German philosophy. The weary, disappointed siblings settled for the winter in Goslar, where they mostly kept to themselves while the locals traded gossip about the strange Englishman lodging with his "sister." Wordsworth, an avid walker, paced the ramparts wrapped in furs and, shivering, composed new poetry.

Wordsworth initially may have thought that Germany would be safe. However, he found himself on the European continent for the first time since his tumultuous experiences in France earlier in the decade. He had been to France twice during the nascent days of the Revolution in 1790 and 1792; he had shared and celebrated the democratic principles that guided the revolutionaries and anticipated eagerly the spread of those principles throughout Europe. This young Wordsworth had championed working-class values, had disdained aristocratic privilege, and had admitted the efficacy of executing Louis XVI. By the time he left England for Germany, however, he was disgusted and disillusioned with the course of the Revolution and had given up France for good. But the violence the French Revolution subsequently aroused during the Terror and then the expansive tyranny of its own militant self-defense made support for the cause untenable. By the time he left England for Germany, having observed all of this with interest, he was disgusted and disillusioned and had given up France for good. In the thirteen-book *Prelude*, he expressed the grotesque irony he saw in the execution of a king only "to crown an Emperor" a decade later, comparing the French embracing of Napoleon to "the dog / Returning to its vomit."[2]

But in 1798 Wordsworth had an even more personal reason to feel emotional duress. Although he was in real terms no closer to France in Goslar than he had been in Somerset, Wordsworth, setting foot on the continent for the first time since 1792, must have felt a symbolic propinquity to his former lover, a Frenchwoman named Annette Vallon, and their daughter, Caroline, whom he had not yet seen.[3] In 1792, Wordsworth, then twenty-two, had returned to England to seek a profession so that he could respectably marry the pregnant Annette; but the outbreak of war between Great Britain and France made it impossible for Wordsworth to return to France. As both English Jacobin and would-be husband, Wordsworth was devastated by the war, then believing his own country to be in the wrong. His despair drove him on foot from London across Salisbury Plain to Tintern Abbey (the first time), where, as he writes five years later upon his return to the spot, he was then "more like a man / Flying from something that he dreads, than one / Who sought the thing he loved."[4] Even when describing the past self, the poet's perspective is always colored by the present one. The now-Wordsworth figures the then-Wordsworth as escaping, but we can be certain of the escapism of only one of them — the one writing.

Years later, adding to *The Prelude*, even as he would face other difficult memories regarding his support for the Revolution, he remains silent on this subject, only hinting at it in the interpolated story of Vaudracour and Julia, a *Romeo and Juliet* knockoff set in France that appears in Book Nine of the thirteen-book *Prelude*. The tale is a rare amorous trifle for Wordsworth and is likely a quasi-autobiographical allegory of his love-life in France. Wordsworth would later extract "Vaudracour and Julia" from *The Prelude* and publish it as a separate poem in 1820, effacing thereafter from his autobiographical poem an ostensibly fictional story and severing it from other memories to which it may have come too close for comfort.

Within only a few weeks of their German sojourn the siblings determined to settle in their native region, the Lake District. This resolution combined with the misery of their current circumstances directed Wordsworth's mind back to the places of his youth and soon to his earliest memories. Writing about his distant memories was a defense against recent ones. For "Tintern Abbey," Wordsworth had written a version of himself in contrast to that more distant recollected self—the desperate one—only a couple of months before he found himself recalling other memories in Goslar. Of course, the trip to Goslar was a kind of escape, too: an escape from reality to the hope of realizable self. Cloistered but without books, Wordsworth was "obliged to write in self-defence," as he explains in a letter to Coleridge in Ratzeburg. "I should have written five times as much as I have done but that I am prevented by an uneasiness at my stomach and side, with a dull pain about my heart." Wordsworth corrects himself, asserting that, instead of "pain," "uneasiness and heat are words which more accurately express my feeling."[5] He was stressed out, in other words, and writing wasn't helping. Feeling the pressure to begin a writing life, the life about to write wasn't so sure he could do it. How could he turn the paralysis of fear into creative action?

During that winter in Goslar, the poet looked inside himself for new material. But he was not certain that what he saw there was worthy of writing, or writing about; and he found weighing the value of it dispiriting. This debilitating anxiety is woven into the fabric of the poem at every stage of its composition and revision—even in its final, published form. The writing of the life in *The Prelude*—in the expanded versions of 1805 and 1839—is predicated on the self having escaped from Goslar: in the thirteen-book version Wordsworth greets the welcome breeze of his native region as a "captive" released from "yon city's walls set free, / A prison where he hath been long immured."[6] For the fourteen-book version Wordsworth is "grateful" to have "escaped / From the vast city, where I long had pined / A discontented sojourner."[7] These opening lines reveal differences between the perspectives of Wordsworth in his early thirties and Wordsworth in his late fifties and early sixties. However, what remains the same is that this escape is, more importantly, an evasion of the paralyzing "trances of thought and mountings of the mind" that the poet must shake off in order to find his subject, to rescue the "chosen son" from his "own unnatural self."[8]

But in the writing for *The Prelude* Wordsworth does in Goslar, during the winter of 1798 to '99, he is not able to shake off those "trances of thought." The potential for creative impotence paradoxically engenders creative production—as it sometimes does, "as by miraculous gift." These "trances of thought" are not Coleridgean reveries that might produce a wonder like "The Ancient Mariner," subtitled in 1800 as "A Poet's Reverie," or the marvelous vision the poet has in "Kubla Khan"; Wordsworth's trances are, instead, potentially cataleptic. The winter months in Goslar were uncomfortable, but what made Wordsworth especially uneasy was the writing—that is, the thinking, the remembering, the ruminating that writing in self-defense required of him. But unpleasant associations abutting him in Goslar no doubt occasioned the "spontaneous overflow of powerful feeling" that Wordsworth describes as being essential to the creation of verse. But what about powerful feelings that one cannot express? Thus, Wordsworth adds the proviso of "emotion recollected in tranquility" to the "spontaneous overflow of powerful feeling" in the preface to *Lyrical Ballads*. But some emotions have no truck with tranquility and assert themselves in anxiety. Feelings and emotions Wordsworth often associates with memory; and remembered feeling is the great gift the mind gives to poetry. But great risks to self and identity come with that potential. Those pesky but pregnant sensitivities may inspire or inhibit writing.

Increasingly, since the composition of "Tintern Abbey," as we have seen, Wordsworth came to associate creativity with memory. Wordsworth found himself relying on memories of home to supply material for composition. The Goslar poems show Wordsworth at work writing *himself* and writing *his self* during the closing months of 1798, sometime between October and December. The "two consciousnesses," the now-Wordsworth and the then-Wordsworth, are again at work. The life writing is asserting its own existence in relation to a fictional, textual self. For the now-Wordsworth, memory is a stimulus to creativity—even when those "mountings of the mind" threaten to quash it—and that creativity finds expression in the relationship between present and past. The creative moment occurs in Wordsworth when the past becomes present in the act of representing memory as past.

As these new poems written in Goslar show, this association involves more a reckoning of one's debts and other costs than of "abundant recompence." The earliest writing for *The Prelude* shows Wordsworth taking account of what he owes, of what he has lost, and of what means he has of paying for it all. That winter the two Wordsworth siblings even shared a notebook because writing was literally too expensive for them due to the cost of paper. Dorothy filled the first several pages with an account of their journey and notes on German grammar. Starting from the opposite end of the notebook, Wordsworth wrote dozens of lines of poetry recto to verso instead of the other way around. The proper order of this scribbling is discernible because he repurposed much of it later for various drafts of what would become *The Prelude*; in fact, Wordsworth preserved some phrases and lines intact throughout the decades of revision to come. Itself a backwards document, the notebook survives as a synecdochic emblem of the process of writing *The*

Prelude. And the fact that it contains Wordsworth's writing literally and materially intertwined with his sister's makes it perhaps even more so.

The Goslar notebook, difficult as it is to follow, reveals Wordsworth's earliest attempts to understand the relationship between memory and creativity for the process of writing *The Prelude.* On the final page of the notebook, facing the inside back cover (on which Wordsworth also has scrawled a few lines), Wordsworth begins his backwards writing with an attempt to figure and thus to understand creativity. The word "inspiration" appears twice at the top of the page, crammed between two attempts to figure out the relationships between the differing meanings of the Latin sense of *inspirare,* literally "to breathe in," as metaphor — "a mild creative breeze," "a gentle inspiration." Although the poem is yet unformed, these early jottings would become the opening of *The Prelude.*[9]

The Goslar jottings are not a recapitulation of "Tintern Abbey" or a prefiguring of the poet's experience with daffodils. What is different? The difference is that peculiarly "redundant energy" — the power that seems so necessary in other poems. His visit to the Wye five years earlier and his discovery of the daffodils seeming to dance in the breeze become transfigured as restorative memories that the imagination somehow knows to call upon when they are needed. But, in the Goslar notebook, Wordsworth is struggling with the spontaneous overflow of these powerful feelings that frustrate his creativity. His exact words in working out just what this "tempest" and "redundant energy" precisely may be are participial: "Creating not but as it may / disturbing things created."[10]

What follows on the page is a list of fragments that redefine it further — "a storm not terrible but / strong / with lights and shades and with / a rushing power / with loveliness and power" — until Wordsworth hits upon the phrase that will persist in revision until the printed *Prelude* half a century later: "trances of thought / And mountings of the mind compared / to which / The wind that drives along th[sic] autumnal lefa[sic] / Is meekness." For the thirteen-book version of *The Prelude*, Wordsworth fastens on that phrase, "Trances of thought and mountings of the mind"; and, as the epigraph to this chapter shows, they "Come fast upon me" as specters of "my own unnatural self."[11]

The "burthen" is memory, bad memories that threaten to ruin everything. But it's not just that the memories conjure negative associations or unpleasant feelings; this burden is "unnatural" because it is from the past, because that self is not the Wordsworth writing the poem. It is a fiction because it does not exist. But the poet *figures* that self anyway (again, as "unnatural"). The former self in Wordsworth tends to be the poet's foil and, at times, the poet's *doppelgänger*. When he came to expand the jottings of Goslar a year later for the two-part *Prelude* of 1799, Wordsworth found no use for the poetry on this page of the notebook — although he would re-work these fragments for subsequent efforts at expanding it. But the Goslar Wordsworth is a liminal self upon which depend the existence of the delineated self and the fixed forms of *The Prelude*.

Those "things created" are not the same "things" as in "Tintern Abbey"; they are, instead, experiences that have already occurred. The "redundant energy" that disturbs them is the creative mind repurposing the memories of those experiences as poetry, articulating them in murmured accents, writing them down as iambic pentameter. It is adaptation. This act is comparable to a film adaptation of a literary work: Wordsworth's originary text is his memory; the poem is his adaptation of that text into a different medium in an attempt to construct a delineated (but not necessarily definitive) self as a new, discrete work.

This is, as he writes further, "a storm not terrible but strong" that has "a rushing power" to produce "trances of thought / And mountings of the mind." Here, it is not clear whether the fragment ("what there is . . .") is a renaming of this rushing power or a counter to it. But, when he re-employs the "trances of thought / And mountings of the mind" he is able to shake off their stymying influence, so he repurposes the phrase as antagonistic.[12] Probably, he does so because, whether he originally intended so or not, the Goslar notebook shows that, on the very next page (again, working backwards), he seems to admonish himself for not being able to shake them off and write the poem he felt destined to write. Wordsworth, in Goslar, is unable to escape from the "burthen" of his "own unnatural self" to embrace his natural self. To do that, he has to go back to the beginning.

Going back to the start, then, in the Goslar notebook, Wordsworth is working backwards in space and thinking backwards in time. On one page near the back of the note-book, Wordsworth has drafted lines toward what would be-come the opening passage of a complete two-part version of *The Prelude* over the next year. The poetry on this page begins seemingly in *medias res*:

> was it for this
> That one, the fairest of all rivers, loved
> To blend his murmurs with my nurse's song
> And from his alder shades and rocky falls,
> And from his fords and shallows sent a voice
> To intertwine my dreams. . . .[13]

The sentiment does seem to follow directly from the frag-ment on the previous page regarding what we might as well go ahead and call writer's block. Wordsworth begins the two-part *Prelude* completed over the next year or so with these lines only slightly emended. And he preserves them for the thirteen- and fourteen-book versions, where they ap-pear in a context that clearly establishes this reading. There, in the preceding lines, Wordsworth presents himself trapped in "listlessness" and "vain perplexity," seeing "Much wanting, so much wanting in myself, / That I recoil and droop." And, like the servant who hides his one talent in Jesus's parable from Matthew 25, Wordsworth is foiled by his own creative inertia, comparing himself to "a false steward who hath much received / And renders nothing back." Breaking the verse paragraph in the midst of the line, after six syllables, the next begins with four that complete the iambic pentameter: "Was it for this[?]" By not writing—probably by not being able to begin the already commissioned (by Coleridge) "Recluse"—Wordsworth feels that he has forsaken the blessing conferred on him by nature as a "chosen son" and judges himself accordingly, in the words of the Gospel, as "wicked and slothful."[14]

So, Wordsworth begins writing *The Prelude* in frustration and self-rebuke. After struggling on the first/last page with the potentially debilitating "trances of thought and mountings of the mind," on the succeeding page (recto, not verso), the first question Wordsworth asks himself is "Was it for this. . . ?" echoing a line from Virgil's *Aeneid* ("*Hoc erat. . . ?*" which literally means something like "Was this all along. . . ?") that became a rhetorical expression of frustration, disappointment, and sarcastic admonishment. In order to further demonstrate Wordsworth's tone, I quote John A. Hodgson's translation of the relevant passage from Virgil:

> Was it for this, fostering parent, that you brought me through spears, through fire?—that I might behold the enemy inside our home, and Ascanius, and my father, and Creusa nearby, slaughtered in each other's blood?[15]

More than twenty years later, Wordsworth himself translated the lines more concisely and with some poetic license: "For this was Priam slain? Troy burnt? The shore / Of Darden seas so often drenched in gore?"[16] In having Aeneas rebuke Venus for not aiding him more directly—basically asking "where were you when I needed you?"—Virgil here imitates Homer's Odysseus expressing similar dismay when Athena appears to him in Book Thirteen of *The Odyssey*. Both protagonists impugn the providential hand that would guide them through such horrors and hardships without intervening to help. In a poem published in the *Morning Post* of January 16, 1799 — contemporaneous with the writing in the Goslar notebook — Robert Southey, friend to Wordsworth and brother-in-law to Coleridge, presents a speaker, like Wordsworth, who proclaims his disgust with the violent course of history. Clio, the classical muse of history, responds by scolding him in the same terms as Aeneas uses to Venus. "O shame! shame!" she cries in "calm anger":

> Was it for this I waken'd thy young mind?
> Was it for this I made thy swelling heart
> Throb at the deeds of Greece, and thy boy's eye
> So kindle when that glorious Spartan died?

The contemporaneity of Wordsworth's and Southey's use of the expression is probably coincidental, as both poets are drawing on a well-established trope. It is the tone established that is important — frustration, disappointment, wrath, despair consonant with feeling destitute of divine favor.

For Wordsworth that favor was bestowed, consecrated by his native river, the Derwent, that still flows behind the Cockermouth house in which he was born. "It" is, to put it simply, the thing, favor, that led to "this," failure. He asks, was I favored only to fail? The river, an agent of Nature, a muse itself perhaps, "loved" to blend its own natural music with the nursery lullabies that formed Wordsworth's creative self. Has he forsaken it? Implicit in this question is another, more formidable and fundamental question — *erat*? It was? Was it? The "it" is more mysterious than the "this" of his failure, even though the antecedent effectively follows with the list of things that were presumably for "this," which is the creative torpor for which the poet is admonishing himself. The rest of *The Prelude* in all its variations strives to understand precisely what "it" is.

Ultimately, however, Wordsworth turns it around. Later, the thirteen- and fourteen-book versions of *The Prelude* open with "O there is a blessing in this gentle breeze." As the breeze passes over his body, Wordsworth feels "within / A corresponding mild creative breeze" in the thirteen-book version and, a catchier variation, "A correspondent breeze" in the fourteen-book version—a blessing indeed but also a powerful metaphor for poetic inspiration.[17] In Book Seven, Wordsworth refers back to these lines as the poem's "glad preamble" characterized by "Dythyrambic fervor."[18] The dithyramb is an ancient Greek lyric form later employed by Pindar and is associated with music and the enthusiastic celebration of Dionysus (Bacchus), the god of wine and fertility and, thus, of sensual pleasures. Looking back at the opening from Book Seven of the thirteen-book *Prelude*, Wordsworth essentially describes the passionate strain that opens the poem as lyric. But, even so, the opening of *The Prelude* also plays upon the tradition of opening the epic poem with an invocation to the muse: he greets the breeze with, "O welcome Messenger! O welcome Friend!" Surprise—the epiclesis, or invocation, of Wordsworth's epic is to Nature! But it is not so much invoked by the poet as it is hailed and received by him as a messenger of new-found liberty and an emblematic friend of the writer.

The point is that the breeze now turns these threatening potentialities into joy, into "dithyrambic fervor." This happens in the later drafts because he has made it home to Grasmere. In a classic essay, M. H. Abrams discusses this opening in relation to the prevalence of the breeze as a metaphor for "radical changes in the poet's mind" in several major poems of the period.[19] Towards the end of the "glad preamble" Wordsworth more specifically explains the metaphor, using key phrases from the Goslar notebook:

For I, methought, while the sweet breath of Heaven
Was blowing on my body, felt within
A corresponding mild creative breeze,
A vital breeze which travelled gently on
O'er things which it had made, and is become
A tempest, a redundant energy
Vexing its own creation.[20]

The creative power is itself so prolific that it threatens—
in its abundant overflow—to undermine its own potential.
The surplus of creativity thwarts or frustrates itself, ham-
pering its own ingenuity and industry. This creative power
is superfluous, excessive and—even more surprising—not
creative, it acts on something already created, not creating
something *sui generis*. In the notebook fragment, this inspiration "passes gently" over the "things which it has [already]
made." This is a power that Wordsworth describes as "creating not" but, instead, as "disturbing things created."[21] In
the later versions of *The Prelude*, Wordsworth explains that
the tempest brings with it "vernal promises" of poetic fertility, while also taxing the poet with the challenge of proving
his "prowess in an honorable field"—the epic poem—and
of being worthy to pursue "The holy life of music and of
verse."[22]

A *Chosen Son*

Why should he grieve? He was a chosen son:
To him was given an ear which deeply felt
The voice of Nature in the obscure wind,
The sounding mountain and the running-stream.[1]

The epic poet is the archetypal literary badass. The difficulty of producing the epic poem is a trope of heroic poetry going back to Homer, wherein the task is so momentous that it requires divine assistance. In the end, the work pays off and guarantees poetic immortality. Of course, the traditional invocation of the Muse is part theatrical performance, part rhetorical flourish as an audacious testament to the awesomeness of the song about to be sung, the poem about to be performed. In the *Inferno* Dante canonizes himself as the sixth greatest poet of all time, with Homer leading the pack. In *Paradise Lost* Milton is bold enough to call upon the same "heav'nly Muse" that inspired Moses to write the Torah and to claim for his poem an "argument / Not less but more heroic" than those of Homer and Virgil.[2] Wordsworth opens the extended *Prelude*, the thirteen- and fourteen-book versions, recalling his return to the Lake District, after the miserable stint in Germany where he began writing it. His tone is ambitious and optimistic, as he remembers feeling the "assurance of some work / Of glory, there forthwith to be begun, / Perhaps, too, there performed."[3]

Well, maybe too optimistic. "Some work of glory" is code for "best epic poem since Milton, or hopefully ever" and thus the phrase is also a sop to Coleridge's ambitions for Wordsworth. The latter is intent, however, on dramatizing the pressure and anxiety in such ambitions. Just as "speedily a longing in me rose / To brace myself to some determined aim, / Reading or thinking," so are those plans

41

quickly usurped by even greater ambitions and formidable obstacles:

> I had hopes
> Still higher, that with a frame of outward life,
> I might endue, might fix in a visible home
> Some portion of those phantoms of conceit
> That had been floating loose about so long,
> And to such Beings temperately deal forth
> The many feelings that oppress'd my heart.
> But I have been discouraged: gleams of light
> Flash often from the East, then disappear
> And mock me with a sky that ripens not
> Into a steady morning: if my mind,
> Remembering the sweet promise of the past,
> Would gladly grapple with some noble theme,
> Vain is her wish; where'er she turns she finds
> Impediments from day to day renew'd.[4]

Sound familiar? "The many feelings that oppress'd my heart" is his expression of the desire to share his experience with readers, to express himself as an artist, trite as that may sound; but what is most pertinent here is the way the writer's ambitions are thwarted by his own insecurity and diffidence. He begins writing precisely to remember "the sweet promise of the past" but finds himself wanting. He finds the "impediments" also in himself. Prefiguring what would be a paraphrase in the preface to *The Excursion*, Wordsworth writes that "When, as becomes a man who would prepare / For such a glorious work, I through myself / Make rigorous inquisition, the report / Is often chearing. . . ." Often cheering, he says, but not always. Still, he feels confident that he possesses or has access to "the vital soul" of creativity and insight, "general truths" and "subordinate helpers of the living mind." Thanks to his upbringing by Nature, and his return home to her, he certainly has the benefit of "external things."

He is also aware that a literary apprenticeship is important, training with words and technique, those "numerous other aids / Of less regard, though won perhaps with toil." He knows that participating in an established literary tradition is "needful to build up a Poet's praise."[5]

The two-book *Prelude* of 1799 has none of this building up of "a Poet's praise." Striking out as an idiosyncratic, potentially innovative, but nonetheless eccentric poet had been the course for *Lyrical Ballads*, which continued to be moderately successful. But this was not the poet of "The Recluse"; stoked by Coleridge's ambitions but always "diffident" of his ability, Wordsworth returns to *The Prelude* early in 1804. Writing about himself was easier this time, and he composed a five-book *Prelude* in about six weeks.[6] But he did not stop there. During this extensive expansion and reworking of the 1799 *Prelude*, Wordsworth decides to go through the motions of writing an epic — using the tradition as either a prompt, conceit, or gimmick. Like Milton does in *Paradise Lost*, Wordsworth reviews potential subjects, including possibly "some old / Romantic tale, by Milton left unsung," or possibly an epic about William Wallace, thus beating Mel Gibson to *Braveheart*.[7] But, again nodding to Coleridge, Wordsworth finds his "last and favorite aspiration" — "some philosophic Song / Of Truth that cherishes our daily life."[8] But he also finds, again, that he is not ready, frozen between ambition and impotence, "with no skill to part / Vague longing that is bred by want of power, / From paramount impulse not to be withstood...."[9] In other words, the spirit is willing, ambition calls him, but he thinks he lacks the strength to bring those "Beings" of the mind, those "phantoms of conceit" into being.

However, when Wordsworth felt the call to follow Milton, he found it easier to write *The Prelude* than to write "The Recluse." At the end of the first book, Wordsworth promises to tell "the story of my life" because "The road lies plain before me" and "'tis a theme / Single and of determined bounds." He adds frankly, "hence / I chuse it rather at this time, than work / Of ampler or more varied argument, / Where I might be discomfited and lost. . . ." Book One closes with the hope that "This labour will be welcome" to Coleridge, "honored Friend."[10] The prospect of surviving a few rounds with Milton, the reigning epic champion, in his own ring in time would become too intimidating and later writers would throw only glancing and sidelong blows effective in their own ways — ranging from Alexander Pope's *The Rape of the Lock* to James Joyce's *Ulysses*. With Coleridge guiding him, Wordsworth's "The Recluse" was to wrest the title from Milton; so Wordsworth wrote *The Prelude* as a warm-up for "The Recluse." More important, the poem on his own life was a dare to himself: Can you do this thing? Are you up to the challenge? Are you really a chosen son?

To meet this challenge, Wordsworth had to imagine a different version of himself from the one imagined by Coleridge. Initially, work towards "The Recluse" runs parallel with writing that would become *The Prelude* as Wordsworth writes away from the image Coleridge had of the poet who would write "The Recluse." *The Prelude*, in a way, begins as an escape from Coleridge's vision of Wordsworth, even as Wordsworth continues to depend on that vision. The figure of the Recluse began with the rustic narrator of "The Ruined Cottage," a peddler whose name in one draft is Armytage, suggesting hermitage. This character quickly evolved into Wordsworth's own fictional versioning of himself as the peddler and eventually developed into the Wanderer of *The Excursion*, which was published in 1814 and would prove to be the only portion of "The Recluse" Wordsworth would complete. Decades later, Wordsworth admitted that the peddler began as a sketch of "what I fancied my own character might have become in his circumstances." Wordsworth's earliest efforts toward expanding "The Ruined Cottage" into a part of this projected "Recluse" are recorded in manuscripts working toward a poem called "The Pedlar." Here, benefit-

ting no doubt from daily literary and philosophical conver-
sations with the sagacious Coleridge, Wordsworth gives his
Pedlar character a background and education among nature
that he would soon repurpose for his own history—not of
a peddler's mind but of a poet's. Wordsworth's original conception, however, depicts a natural genius developed only
through the minimal education of a boy intended for a shep-
herd's occupation but also through extensive communion
with Nature:

> Though he was untaught,
> In the dead lore of schools undisciplined,
> Why should he grieve? He was a chosen son:
> To him was given an ear which deeply felt
> The voice of Nature in the obscure wind,
> The sounding mountain and the running stream.
> To every natural form, rock, fruit, and flower,
> Even the loose stones that cover the highway,
> He gave a moral life; he saw them feel
> Or linked them to some feeling. In all shapes
> He found a secret and mysterious soul,
> A fragrance and a spirit of strange meaning.[11]

In these lines, written weeks before the poet's second visit
to the Wye, and the subsequent composition of "Tintern
Abbey," Wordsworth found himself in the Pedlar.

Through the process of inventing a fictional character, he
recognized himself in the reflection as that "chosen son" of
Nature. In another fragment of "The Pedlar," Wordsworth
inscribes the character's experience of the world with his
trademark pantheism, partly developed from Coleridge's
metaphysical speculations:

> Wonder not
> If such his transports were for in all things
> He saw one life & felt that it was joy

> One song they sang and it was audible
> Most audible then when the fleshly ear,
> O'ercome by grosser prelude of that strain,
> Forgot its functions, & slept undisturbed.

The Pedlar, trained in his perceptions by a "bliss ineffable" bestowed on him by Nature, can hear the empirically inaudible song sung by all natural things that supersedes as transcendental echo the previously heard "grosser prelude." At the risk of making too much of a coincidence, this passage includes the first usage of the word "prelude" in Wordsworth's poetry. The lines here describing the Pedlar figure precisely Wordsworth's conception of *The Prelude* as the overture to the symphony of his body of work. The influence of Nature's "overflowing soul" on his intellect is "so much," he writes of the Pedlar, "that all his thoughts / Were steeped in feeling."[12]

"Feeling," too, is an essential concept in Wordsworth, not to be confused with trite expressions of sensibility or effusions of emotion, for the Wordsworthian capacity for feeling is trained by the intellect and its auxiliary functions — perception, memory, and imagination, which are not discretely functioning but, rather, coordinative powers. The Pedlar apprehends through feeling "the sentiment of being, spread / O'er all that moves, & all that seemeth still" and understands all that is "lost beyond the reach of thought / And human knowledge," all that is "to the human eye / Invisible, yet liveth to the heart."[13] In these lines Wordsworth finds not only himself but something akin to transcendentalism that he is able to adapt as a poetics for writing himself. Within a few months, Wordsworth would change the third-person pronouns to first-person pronouns for the first complete draft of his poem to Coleridge — the Pedlar, a concept developed in collaboration with Coleridge, having been, in more ways than one, the antecedent for the self Wordsworth writes in *The Prelude*. Wordsworth, returning from Germany, would adapt the lines and phrases quoted above, written before leaving for Germany, as descriptive, not of the Pedlar, but of himself. For the two-part *Prelude*, he changed the third-person pronouns to first-person ones.[14]

Wordsworth calls himself "a chosen Son" in Book Three of *The Prelude*. In sharp contrast to the Pedlar, however, he does it when he describes his freshman year at college. Surrounded by privilege, Wordsworth at Cambridge found himself abashed by his country accent, humiliated by his duties as a sizar (akin to a work-study student), intimidated by the competitive spirit among his fellows, and haunted by the shades of those distinguished alumni, Milton and Newton. The poet's first year at Cambridge threatened to subdue his "visionary mind."[15] Wordsworth was not the last creative type to find his college education uninspiring and potentially stultifying. But he did broaden and deepen his literary knowledge by surreptitiously reading Chaucer and Spenser, who were less intimidating Cambridge affiliates, and not on the approved reading list. Wordsworth would disappoint his family by graduating without distinction. A prototypical English major, he couldn't meet the demands of the Newtonian mathematics curriculum.

Wordsworth writes that, at Cambridge, he feels displaced because he is unlike the other young men. He describes "a strangeness in my mind, / A feeling that I was not for that hour, / Nor for that place." Strikingly, he adapts lines written for the Pedlar to describe himself at Cambridge, putting them into a different context:

> Why should I grieve? I was a chosen Son.
> For hither I had come with holy powers
> And faculties, whether to work or feel:
> To apprehend all passions and all moods
> Which time, and place, and season do impress
> Upon the visible universe; and work
> Like changes there by force of my own mind.[16]

The younger Wordsworth thinks he already has all the education he needs; the past perfect ("I had come") indicates the ironic distance between that young man and the life writing. The Pedlar, moreover, never would have gone to Cambridge. But Wordsworth wanted some of the Pedlar for himself and that part of himself envies the Pedlar for not having to follow this course.

In this weird conflation of a fictional character with a bad experience, Wordsworth finds an ideal image of himself and hears his poetic calling. During the "Summer Vacation" described in Book Four, Wordsworth is back home among the lakes, fells, and crags. Whereas the Pedlar is destined to be a rustic philosopher, Wordsworth finds a slightly different course for himself. One early morning, after a night of carousing (Wordsworth?!), his destiny is revealed to him: preserving the mystery of what Kenneth R. Johnston calls the "Dawn Dedication," he gratefully exclaims to Coleridge,

> —Ah! need I say, dear Friend, that to the brim
> My heart was full; I made no vows, but vows
> Were then made for me; bond unknown to me
> Was given, that I should be, else sinning greatly,
> A dedicated Spirit. On I walk'd
> In blessedness which even yet remains.[17]

When he returns to his "unlovely Cell" at Cambridge he is "detached / Internally from academic cares." He has resolved "to be a lodger in that house / Of Letters, and no more" but is still diffident of his powers.[18] By the time he completes his degree, his poetic vocation is fully upon him, and he thinks he "might leave / Some monument behind me which pure hearts / Should reverence."[19] He has begun to conceptualize his history as an epic—possibly without fully realizing it as an innovative variation on the tradition that can make a Homer, a Virgil, or a Milton. Ironically, by rewriting the Pedlar as himself in a different context, he retroactively applies, on his own terms, at least part of Coleridge's image of himself in the mystical communion that confirms his destiny.

Picking up on the notion first associated with the Pedlar, Wordsworth begins to adapt the figure of the chosen son for himself in the autobiographical fragments he jots down in the Goslar notebook. In lines Wordsworth dictated to his sister, he posits what will become the thesis of his entire life, the biological and the poetical:

> I believe
> That there are spirits which when they would form
> A favor'd being open out the clouds
> As at the touch of lightning
> Seeking him with gentle visitation. . . .[20]

Even in the first drafts of *The Prelude* dating from 1798, Wordsworth recognizes — with more gratitude than pride — that he was "a favor'd being." The being already exists — but he is not formed yet as a "favor'd being" until the spirits find him and consummate their will with "gentle visitation." Wordsworth envisions other spirits, "aiming at the self-same end" as these but who "use . . . Severer interventions" and "ministry / Of grosser kind." He asserts that "of their school was I."[21] His schooling by these spirits is the main subject of the first book of the two-book *Prelude*. But Wordsworth first must figure himself as a "favor'd being" in order for the admonishment of the "was it for this" passage to carry its weight. But this figuring of "the years of unrememberable being," immemorial existence, the writing of one's essential self, is also the way around — if not effectually the way out of — the paralysis brought about by the pressure to write "The Recluse."

A few months later, when he begins developing fragments of verse into the two-part *Prelude*, he frames the passage differently, nearly as a *non sequitur*: after describing some of his earliest memories, Wordsworth pauses abruptly to explain, "The mind of man is fashioned & built up / Even as a strain of music. . . ."[22] It is significant that Wordsworth's first pass at this idea in the Goslar notebook suggests an equivalence or a parellelism between the mind and the soul: "The soul of man is fashioned & built up / Just like a strain of music." Wordsworth obviously was experimenting in thought with the possibility that our very soul is housed within the mind as a function of, or a power coordinate with, the imagination. But the substitution of "mind" for "soul" in the next draft suggests that Wordsworth sees the soul in more essentialist terms—as the neo-Platonism of the "Intimations" ode also indicates. The mind, however, must be able to grow—the poem records the "growth" of a poet's mind. As a "history of a Poet's mind," implying a *telos*, therefore Wordsworth's primary interest in *The Prelude* is "the mind of man," specifically a man-poet, but what does it mean for the mind to be fashioned even "as a strain of music"? Does he mean that the mind is fashioned as a strain of music is fashioned? Or that the mind is made to be similar to a strain of music? In order for something to be fashioned it must already exist as something that can be made into something else, so I tend to favor the former meaning. Wordsworth goes on to emphasize the fashioning in the subsequent lines, where he describes the "gentle visitation" of the spirits who command that process of making into being or, more accurately, into action. Those visitations extend the melody. And they visit everyone, Wordsworth goes on to assert. These are "quiet powers" that are "retired, and seldom recognized, yet kind, / And to the very meanest not unknown." By "meanest" Wordsworth means the most ordinary people, although the double negative makes the sentiment seem a bit stinting (the British love ironic litotes). But Wordsworth writes that these spirits "rarely" communed with him as a boy. Other spirits "aiming at the self-same end"—that is, the making of a "favored being"—administer the "severer interventions" first developed in the Goslar notebook but which is now "ministry / More palpable" than the "gentle visitation" of the former spirits.[23] But what does this have to do with music? The fashioning. For example, when he revised the above passage for the thirteen-book version, Wordsworth has decided on the second reading proposed above, asserting that

> The mind of Man is framed even like the breath
> And harmony of music. There is a dark
> Invisible workmanship that reconciles
> Discordant elements, and makes them move
> In one society.[24]

Now, the "workmanship" reminds us of the unknown workman, the dark, unseen, and invisible subject doing the action of the passive verbs — "is fashioned," "[is] built up," and now "is framed." While still figurative language (obviously), "to frame" is a more workmanlike, less effete verb that connotes the hard work involved in building a poet's mind, possibly still synonymous with his soul. And while the musical metaphor continues with "Discordant" Wordsworth deliberately, it seems, mixes it by expressing harmony ultimately as "society," strengthening the image of work being done by constituents (workers, tones) to make a whole. The dissonant tones that are pushed to resolution as part of a larger matrix. It's kind of like jazz — or a Wagnerian overture that prefigures the *Liebestod*.

For the thirteen- and the fourteen-book versions, Wordsworth would clarify just in what those "severer interventions" consist. "Fair seed-time had my soul," Wordsworth explains, "and I grew up / Fostered alike by beauty and by fear."[25] By "fear" he means "awe" — so that his most formative experience of nature is akin to what Edmund Burke writes about in his *Philosophical Enquiry into the Origin of Our Ideas of the Sublime and Beautiful*. But instead of enabling the devel-

opment of an aesthetic, the sublime and beautiful nurture
Wordsworth's poetic. In all three versions of *The Prelude*,
Wordsworth describes the now-famous episode in which he
as a boy rows out on Ullswater in a stolen skiff; haunted by
guilt, he believes the mountains to be pursuing him. After-
wards, Wordsworth writes that "for many days, my brain /
Worked with a dim and undetermined sense / Of unknown
modes of being." In other words, he becomes aware, due
to the "severer interventions" of those other spirits, of the
thingness of those Wordsworthian things. It sounds like
an epiphany of Platonic idealism but it disturbs him in the
same way as the creative power he elsewhere describes as
"disturbing things created": "huge and mighty Forms that
do not live / Like living men moved slowly through my
mind / By day, and were the trouble of my dreams." He is
the created thing that is transformed into something else.
These experiences teach him about "high objects," "enduring things," and "grandeur in the beatings of the heart."[26]
Previously discordant notes fall into harmony as the boy
gradually coheres into a more deeply thinking and feeling
man. The mind and the soul are confirmed to be one in the
same. In the thirteen-book *Prelude*, having replaced "fashioned and built up" with "framed," Wordsworth repurposes
the idea by explaining that the invisible workman, the dark
composer, is nothing less than the "Wisdom and Spirit of
the universe! Thou Soul that art the Eternity of Thought!"
This seeminginly transcendent entity that is actually an im-
manent one turns out to be the subject of the verb: "from
my first dawn / Of Childhood didst Thou intertwine for
me / The passions that *build up* our human Soul." The emphasis is mine but the religious timbre is Wordsworth's. But
whose "human Soul"? "Our"? A "poet is a man speaking
to men," after all, but couldn't it be that "our human Soul"
is shared by all of us with the "Wisdom and Spirit of the
universe," making a direct line from "our human Soul" to
that "Soul that art the Eternity of Thought"? Wordsworth is

of course the musican making the music here, but this recursive figuring of creativity is essential to the life writing because Wordsworth has to first imagine and then create a musician making the music that makes him.

Still, an interlocutor (again, himself) challenges him: Why should anybody (other than Coleridge) care about your odyssey? Especially if you can't write the great philosophical epic? As early as 1805 Wordsworth referred to *The Prelude* figuratively as "a sort of portico to the Recluse."[27] In his 1814 preface to *The Excursion* Wordsworth is still thinking of the autobiographical poem in relation to the larger epic project, describing the proportions of one to the other as analogous to the architectural relationship "the Anti-chapel [or ante-chapel] has to the body of a gothic church." In this preface, Wordsworth also writes that the poem on "the origin and progress of his own powers . . . has long been finished" but implies that it will appear only when all of his poems "shall be properly arranged," presumably by the poet himself at some future time when "The Recluse" is complete.[28] Wordsworth had decided a decade before that *The Prelude* would never appear in print "till another work has been written and published, of sufficient importance to justify me in giving my own history to the world." He goes on to express the doubt, hope, and anxiety that characterizes the relationship between *The Prelude* and what Wordsworth perceived to be a greater poetic calling: "I pray God to give me life to finish these works which I trust will live and do good, especially the one, to which that I have been speaking of as so far advanced is only supplementary."[29] Wordsworth intended to publish *The Prelude* only after completing "The Recluse" because only then would he feel confident that readers would take any interest in what he might have to say about the development of his poetical powers. Thus he asserts in a letter to Thomas De Quincey that the "Poem on my own earlier life . . . will not be published these many years, and never during my lifetime, till I have finished a

larger and more important work to which it is tributary."
Wordsworth adds, "To this work ['The Recluse'] I mean
to devote the Prime of my life and the chief force of my
mind."[30] Wordsworth failed to realize that the "preparatory," "supplementary," "tributary" poem he was at that time
in the midst of writing was the most original contribution
to the epic tradition since Milton and would be the last successful epic poem ever written.

So, we can think of *The Prelude* as an epic poem about not
being able to write an epic poem. Perhaps this is due to its
delinquent muse (Coleridge). But epics also require heroes.
Even as he fretted over writing "The Recluse" and besting
Milton in the epic arena, Wordsworth found in himself the
subject best suited for his skills. Wordsworth felt he had to
write a great work that would be important to the world, but
he didn't know where to begin or really what to say. So, he
began writing about himself—he becomes those "Beings,"
he impersonates "those phantoms of conceit." Throughout
The Prelude, often calling Coleridge to witness and to verify
it, Wordsworth pauses to marvel at what he is doing and
to give thanks for what he with sincere humility calls "the
glory of my youth."[31] Wordsworth shows this writer in the
process of adapting memories of his past for the purposes
of the writing moment in process. This is partly why Wordsworth couldn't publish it; he couldn't stop revising it because he was always writing himself as the living organic
being who resides there in that moment of remembering
and representing.

And no one ever wrote an epic who did not believe
himself to be "a chosen son." The model of the epic and
its modes of adaptation and transmutation provide Wordsworth with a way of thinking about his own history, freeing
him to adapt his personal history and his poetic identity to
suit his writing needs in the act of creating. In Book Four,
Wordsworth analogizes the progress backwards through
memory in his poem with the slow progress one makes in a

boat across shallow still water. Fittingly, he does so using an epic simile (that is, a really long simile), a standard convention since Homer, to emphasize this as taking place in the writing moment happening now — which also happens to be the reading moment:

> As one who hangs, down-bending from the side
> Of a slow-moving Boat, upon the breast
> Of a still water, solacing himself
> With such discoveries as his eye can make,
> Beneath him, in the bottom of the deeps,
> Sees many beauteous sights, weeds, fishes, flowers,
> Grots, pebbles, roots of trees, and fancies more;
> Yet often is perplexed, and cannot part
> The shadow from the substance, rocks and sky,
> Mountains and clouds, from that which is indeed
> The region, and the things which there abide
> In their true dwelling; now is crossed by gleam
> Of his own image, by a sunbeam now,
> And motions that are sent he knows not whence,
> Impediments that make his task more sweet;
> — Such pleasant office have we long pursued,
> Incumbent o'er the surface of past time
> With like success; nor have we often looked
> On more alluring shows (to me, at least,)
> More soft, or less ambiguously descried,
> Than those which now we have been passing by,
> And where we still are lingering.[32]

This long passage is a lovely example of how following the rules of form, genre, or mode can produce good writing. If Wordsworth is playing by the rules of the game, he knows he's got to have an epic simile somewhere — it's on the epic poet's to-do list. The simile is first a figure for memory but it ends up being a simile for the poet's writing of the poem for someone to read; the poet's inclusion of the implied reader with him, "we," emphasizes the imaginative and self-consciously literary work of the poet in the simile, from the one on the boat who "fancies" he sees more than he does to the reader's participation in its effectiveness. The boat, and the poem, course "o'er the surface of past time," paradoxical progress backwards that began in the Goslar notebook. The boat is presumably moving towards a shore, its bourn. But even the future anticipated in the poem, again as suggested by its being a "prelude" to something, is only the creative work of the imaginative moment.

The epic mode also makes what Wordsworth is doing self-consciously literary and facilitates the expression of this version of himself/his self to Coleridge via a shared literary language. After the "preamble" (which makes an illuminating comparison with Milton's proemium, the first 26 lines of *Paradise Lost*) the poet gets around to invoking Coleridge, "O Friend!", as the muse-proper of *The Prelude*.[33] The epic is always about the poet's power—invoked or otherwise—but *The Prelude* begins with the poet already in possession of the power. He wants to know where it really comes from—not a from a mystical muse, but from the formative experiences of his life—"Of Genius, Power, Creation and Divinity itself / I have been speaking, for my theme has been / What passed within me." Here Wordsworth finds the theme of "The Recluse"—"the might of Souls" and the inner life of all humankind. "This is, in truth," he writes echoing Milton, "heroic argument." But he has not words to develop this epic theme, making only "Breathings for incommunicable powers" because he cannot enter into the souls and experiences of others: "Yet each man is a memory to himself." But Wordsworth does know "there's not a man / That lives who hath not had his godlike hours."[34] (One suspects that had he written "The Recluse" it might have had an ethical stance anticipating the ideas of Husserl and Levinas.) However, just as he recognizes this intersubjectivity, he retreats back into himself, into an egocentric viewpoint. But epic.

Implicitly comparing himself to Odysseus, Wordsworth writes, "A Traveller I am, / And all my Tale is of myself." If this epic's muse is Coleridge, then what Wordsworth invokes is the muse as partner, collaborator, mentor: "Thou, O honored Friend! / Who in my thoughts art ever at my side, / Uphold, as heretofore, my fainting steps."[35] Coleridge, then, is also like Athena looking out for Odysseus, setting up certain challenges for him to overcome, to demonstrate his worthiness. At times, he is Athena in disguise as Mentor guiding Telemakhos towards *kleos*, or "fame on the lips of men." A potent allusion at the opening of the thirteen- and the fourteen-book *Prelude* specifies that *Paradise Lost* indeed haunts the poet's ambition: acknowledging his liberty from "a house / Of bondage," Wordsworth declares, "The earth is all before me," thus echoing the conclusion of *Paradise Lost* where Adam and Eve, leaving Eden, understand that "The world was all before them."[36] In a sense, *The Prelude* picks up where *Paradise Lost* leaves off, with Wordsworth as a new Adam at liberty to choose the means by which he may regain Paradise. *The Prelude* is the virtual sequel to *Paradise Lost*.

This was not enough for Coleridge, however. Although he was disappointed in Wordsworth for writing *The Prelude* instead of "The Recluse," Coleridge approved of it more than he did of *The Excursion*, which Wordsworth intended to be the "second part" of "The Recluse." In private, however, Coleridge was more profoundly disappointed in Wordsworth than he expresses in the *Biographia Literaria*. Upon reading *The Excursion*, Coleridge compared it unfavorably to *The Prelude*, writing, "I do not think, I did not feel, it equal to the Work on the Growth of his own spirit."[37] He communicated his disappointment to Wordsworth directly in an excruciating letter that explains in great detail what he was expecting, where Wordsworth had gotten it all wrong, and what he should have done instead. Confusingly, at least for Wordsworth, Coleridge faults *The Excursion* for not being the poem to which *The Prelude* was supposed to be the prelude and sees no fruitful connection between *The Prelude* and *The Excursion* and thus no hope for "The Recluse." Coleridge ruefully adds, "Whatever in Lucretius is Poetry is not philosophical, whatever is philosophical is not Poetry: and in the very Pride of confident Hope I looked forward to the Recluse, as the *first* and *only* true Phil[osophical] Poem in existence."[38]

Strangely, though, Lucretius probably suits Wordsworth better than Shakespeare or Milton do. Although he never became the philosophical poet that Coleridge wanted him to be, Wordsworth was interested in metaphysics. His thinking about such matters tends to focus on how they relate to identity and self. He comes up with a subjective metaphysics associated with poetics, with making, with creating—both poetry and identity. Wordsworth's chief subject—even before Wordsworth himself—is the poem itself as a poem about the development of the writerly self. And that making requires investigation of the writer's poetic vision, of ontology—all so that he might "construct a literary Work that might live." Writing about his life and writing for his afterlife became discrete but psychically inextricable undertakings. This is why in the "Intimations" ode Wordsworth is so worried about the potential degeneration of the writer's poetic vision, his creativity.

By the end of it, Coleridge, the ideal reader of *The Prelude*, is himself remade, reborn, awake in an attitude of prayer—according to his own account. Over the course of several evenings, Coleridge literally did hear Wordsworth "talk so much about himself" during an epic recitation of *The Prelude*. He described it as a "philosophico-biographical Poem" and, flattered and impressed by it, composed his own tribute to it in 1807.[39] There he celebrates Wordsworth as "friend," "teacher," "comforter," "guide," and "God's great Gift to me!"[40] Wordsworth's poem clearly had its intended effect, for Coleridge describes himself in Wordsworthian terms at the conclusion of the reading—"I sate, my Being blended in one Thought . . . / And when I rose, I found myself in Prayer!"[41] The fact that Coleridge even finished the poem is a testament to his deeply personal response and his admiration for the work. Wordsworth asked Coleridge not to publish his response because he was uncomfortable with the poem's praise for a work that was unpublished and, to his mind, unfinished. Coleridge did anyway—probably out of spite.

There was a Boy

There was a Boy, ye knew him well, ye Cliffs
And Islands of Winander! many a time,
At evening, when the stars had just begun
To move along the edges of the hills,
Rising or setting, would he stand alone,
Beneath the trees, or by the glimmering lake,
And there, with fingers interwoven, both hands
Press'd closely palm to palm and to his mouth
Uplifted, he, as through an instrument,
Blew mimic hootings to the silent owls
That they might answer him.[1]

There *was* a boy, and it used to be Wordsworth. Literally, figuratively, textually. The boy of Winander (or, as the place is known today, Windermere) in the untitled poem from the 1800 *Lyrical Ballads*—the first passage from *The Prelude* to appear in print—was originally a description of the poet's youth, written, again, in the Goslar notebook. The first eleven lines above comprise the poem's first complete sentence and describe the boy's playing outdoors, culminating in his memorable "mimic hootings" to the owls. The poem goes on to describe the owls' "responsive" call, emphasizing the interrelatedness between the child and nature. The first verse paragraph concludes with the mysterious and ominous implication that the boy hears something more profound in moments of silence that seems to be allegorized by the "uncertain heaven" reflected in the lake. When Coleridge read the poem, sent no later than the end of November 1798 in a letter from Goslar, he responded, "had I met these lines running wild in the deserts of Arabia, I should have instantly screamed out 'Wordsworth!'"[2] Coleridge recognized certainly the poem and probably the boy in it as the projected author of "The Recluse."

While this boy may indeed have been a "favor'd being," the boy in the Goslar notebook is clearly Wordsworth. There, after the lines introducing the boy in the third-person, Wordsworth, perhaps unconsciously, slips into first-person pronouns to describe his own hooting at the owls: the first drafting of the lines I used as the epigraph above read,

> When the stars began
> To move along the edges of the hills
> Rising or setting would he stand alone
> Beneath the trees or by the glimmering lakes
> And through his fingers woven in one close knot
> Blow mimic hoot[ings] to the silent owls
> And bid them answer him. And they would shout
> Across the watry[sic] vale & shout again
> Responsive to my call. . . .³

Subtly enough for sure, Wordsworth has either revealed himself to be the boy or has, through the act of writing, become the boy. What remains of this fragmentary draft remains in the first person as Wordsworth seemingly recalls the same sort of mystical communion with nature that characterizes the youth of his "Pedlar" character:

> And when it chanced
> That pauses of deep silence mockd[sic] my skill
> Then, often, in that silence while I hung
> Listening a sudden shock of mild surprise
> Would carry far into my heart the voice
> Of mountain torrents: or the visible scene
> Would enter unawares into my mind
> With all its solemn imagery[:] its rocks
> Its woods & that uncertain heaven receved[sic]
> Into the bosom of the steady lake⁴

The fragment ends here. In "The Pedlar," Wordsworth describes a similar interaction between nature and his six-year-old protagonist; the boy's experience of physical nature engenders a purely spiritual existence that "swallow'd up / His animal being." "In such access of mind," Wordsworth writes, "in such high hour / Of visitation from the living God, / Thought was not."[5] Wordsworth wants to believe that what he describes has been true for him. Writers can always obviate ontological uncertainty by casting themselves as fictional characters.

Or they end up exacerbating it. These lines from the notebook about the boy of Winander remain generally unchanged when the poem appears in *Lyrical Ballads* and then in all of the longer versions of *The Prelude* through to publication. The only major difference is that the first-person pronouns above are revised as third-person pronouns—"the visible scene / Would enter unawares into his mind. . . ."[6] In the ensuing lines that Wordsworth added starting with the 1800 *Lyrical Ballads*, however, he makes the surprising decision to kill the boy he had first written as himself and then presents himself as a meditative visitor to his grave:

> And there along that bank when I have pass'd
> At evening, I believe, that near his grave
> A full half-hour together I have stood
> Mute——for he died when he was ten years old.[7]

Here, and later in *The Prelude*, the final sentence and section of the poem/passage shifts to a juxtaposition of the boy's birthplace and burial-place, then concludes with an emphasis on the "mute" poet in silent contemplation of the boy's untimely death. The passage appears as a transition from the polemic to recollections of the poet's childhood days. Wordsworth adds that the "boy was taken from his mates" for an unspecified reason, perhaps illness, emphasizing the likelihood of the boy having been one of Words-

worth's classmates at Hawkshead Grammar School. However, in any reading of the lines in context, the "mates" could
only be the owls. It is a composite of Wordsworth and his
schoolboy friends, but it is also an intensely subjective experience that Wordsworth recalls, describes, invents here —
one that carries with it the sense of authoritative autobiography. In an interview, Wordsworth cites one lad in particular
as excelling in the "mimic hootings."[8] School records reveal,
moreover, that a classmate did die in 1782, when Wordsworth was twelve years old. In the final edits of what would
become *The Prelude*, Wordsworth changes the age of the
boy at his death from ten to twelve.[9] This last section of the
poem/passage complicates our understanding of the Goslar
poetry because what would have been an autobiographical
fragment for *The Prelude* becomes the poet musing upon a
version of himself now dead. Regardless of who really was
the best mimic or who actually died, what is important here
is the way the "visible scene / Would enter unawares into
his mind / With all its solemn imagery." If the boy is not
Wordsworth then he is like Wordsworth and, had he lived,
this "chosen son" would have become a poet.

But the boy of Winander does not become anything but
part of the poet's poem about his own becoming. As such,
the boy from the past supposedly had being but only one becoming, only one transformative moment of preternatural
quickening as he pauses for the owls' responses. And Wordsworth makes the boy the grammatical object of the significant actions in the poem — the natural things, as subjects,
perform their actions upon him. He is passive in his limi-
nality, in his moment of becoming. The writing of one's self
necessarily involves a sorting of verbs, their tenses, moods,
and aspects. It has everything to do with what was, what
is, what has been, what is being. In writing everything is;
nothing can not be. It is only that memory that fools us
into thinking that something used to be and now no longer
exists.

Naturally, Wordsworth's "history of a poet's mind" explores his childhood but also his remarkable ontology of childhood—which is, also naturally, an ontology of creativity and the poetic imagination. In the second book of the thirteen-book *Prelude* Wordsworth, without using the phrase, speculates on the "years of unrememberable being"—or, as he admits parenthetically, "with my best conjectures I would trace / The progress of being" from the intimate relationship between the infant and its mother. This condition, by which the "infant Babe" is daily "Subjected to the discipline of love," is a Lockean overload of sensations shaping the mind that is itself "Tenacious of the forms which it receives." But soon something else takes over—something we might rather call "Blakean" than "Lockean"—as the creative imagination establishes its inevitable connection with the "active principle" discussed above. "Emphatically such a being lives," Wordsworth writes, describing the powerful instinct for survival while also claiming the infant as "An inmate of this active universe." The basic emotions enhance the creative faculty in their vigorous assertiveness as the child begins to understand—and, by understanding, to invent—the world:

> his mind,
> Even as an agent of the one great mind,
> Creates, creator and receiver both,
> Working but in alliance with the works
> Which it beholds.——Such verily is the first
> Poetic spirit of our human life. . . .[10]

The infant exists in a purely empirical state of consciousness, without doubt, while the influence of the mother's nurturing on the infant's rapidly developing mind establishes an ontology of love founded on the imagined and imaginative bond. Wordsworth has realized that he was prepared to have an experience like the one he had near Tintern Abbey with

Dorothy at his side because of his first experience of love, which is itself a powerfully imaginative activity. This is key for Wordsworth's poetry because it is the fact that we all share the same poetic spirit that, he hopes, will make his poetry valuable to others.

As in the "Intimations Ode," however, this poetic spirit, its universality notwithstanding, is not sustainable in most people for the same reasons, the "uniform controul" of daily life, its stultifying banality. In the ode, through social-ization and maturity the adult loses the poetic vision as it fades with age, with the accumulation of experience. As in Blake's poetry, the perspective of childhood, its innocence, is threatened by the perverted perspective of experience. While Wordsworth's vision of adulthood is not as grim as Blake's, coming from him it feels more depressing. But, in *The Prelude* there is hope for some, in whom the poetic spirit, "Through every change of growth or of decay," re-mains "Pre-eminent till death."[11] Because he is so interested in life, Wordsworth is also, like Dickens later, committed to understanding and to celebrating the experience of chil-dren—that is, the being and becoming involved therein.[12] Famously, in the "Intimations" ode, Wordsworth lauds the child as the "best Philosopher."[13] I have a colleague in phi-losophy who makes fun of Wordsworth for conferring such a distinction on children, but Wordsworth is not claiming that the child is a superior metaphysician. Wordsworth is being literal, employing the original denotation from the Greek *philosophia*; the child simply loves learning, loves the acquiring of experience, of wisdom, even as it may be an un-sophisticated wisdom. Childhood is profoundly empirical even as it is also unreasonable, or not yet rational.

In a short lyric, Wordsworth proclaims, "The child is the father of the man"—a position he expounds upon in both the "Intimations" ode and *The Prelude*.[14] In the thirteen-book version of *The Prelude*, which is roughly contem-poraneous with the ode, Wordsworth is working out an understanding of the value of childhood experience as a foundation for whatever wisdom the adult may possess. Wordsworth is grateful for the ignorance and uncertainty that provokes curiosity and incites wisdom — "those obstinate questionings / Of sense and outward things, / Fallings from us, vanishings; / Blank misgivings of a Creature / Moving about in worlds not realized. . . ."[15] In *The Prelude*, around one hundred lines beyond where he placed the boy of Winander passage, Wordsworth writes, adducing the "solemn imagery" that interpenetrates the boy's mind as well as his own childhood reading of fantasy books:

> Our simple childhood sits upon a throne
> That hath more power than all the elements.
> I guess not what this tells of Being past,
> Nor what it augurs of the life to come;
> But so it is. . . .[16]

Ironically, in the longer version of the ode, Wordsworth is less circumspect than in the poem that would remain unpublished for decades: "Not in entire forgetfulness, / And not in utter nakedness," Wordsworth writes of our birth in the ode, "But trailing clouds of glory do we come / From God, who is our home."[17] Here, he posits the Platonic notion of the pre-existence of the soul that he explained later was not so much a spiritual conviction as it was a poetic device.[18] The child does not empirically experience the world in a Lockean sense but "read'st" it and thus knows a Platonic truth that will eventually fade. Wordsworth likely is being deliberately provocative of Enlightenment epistemology in favor of something like Christian transcendence. But it is a transcendence that is weighted down and oppressed by the mundane concerns of adulthood, what Wordsworth calls "custom"; it is "Heavy as frost." But, as he asserts, we grow away from that light, "our Life's star," which is equivalent to one's ontological essence, the soul itself, as we get older: "Shades of the prison-house begin to close / Upon the growing Boy" and darken his perception of his divine origin. And eventually "the Man perceives it die away, / And fade into the light of common day."[19] Possibly because of the role urged on him by Coleridge, Wordsworth as a public philosopher had to speak with greater confidence than was called for in his more private writing.

Wordsworth's preface to his 1815 collected *Poems* contains some useful commentary on poetry and imagination. It is generally less polemical and pompous than the preface to *Lyrical Ballads* (and far more readable!). What is also particularly interesting about this volume is that Wordsworth makes the first of many attempts to categorize his assorted works by theme and genre. He creates such rubrics as "Poems Referring to the Period of Childhood," which opens the collection, and "Poems Referring to the Period of Old Age" and "Epitaphs and Elegiac Poems," poems associated with death, which, preceding the concluding "Intimations" ode, close the collection. Following Coleridge's lead, Wordsworth makes a distinction between his "Poems of the Fancy" and his "Poems of the Imagination." Guess who leads the latter series? The boy of Winander. But even here, where the boy dies as usual, Wordsworth admits in the preface that he is "one of my own primary consciousnesses"—that is, as he writes elsewhere, his former self, "some other Being." The poem belongs there, he asserts, because it represents "a commutation and transfer of internal feelings, co-operating with external accidents to plant, for immortality, images of sound and sight, in the celestial soil of the Imagination." It is the birth in the boy—the rebirth?—of "the active principle." So, why does he die? Wordsworth is mum. But this boy, lacking being, presumably is deprived of "the faculty exerting itself upon various objects of the external universe," the subject of the succeeding poems in the series.[20] Even if being never becomes, it does at last cease to be.

shrines so Frail

Oh! why hath not the mind
Some element to stamp her image on
In nature somewhat nearer to her own?
Why, gifted with such powers to send abroad
Her spirit, must it lodge in shrines so frail?[1]

Like "There Was a Boy," many of the new poems Wordsworth wrote in Germany appeared in the two-volume *Lyrical Ballads* of 1800, the greatly expanded second edition of the book originally published in collaboration with Coleridge two years earlier. The first volume is a reordering of the 1798 edition, which includes "Tintern Abbey" and Coleridge's "Ancient Mariner." Coleridge's confidence in Wordsworth's greatness and attendant sense of his own inferiority became his excuse for failing to contribute his share of poetry for the second edition: Coleridge announced in 1800, "I abandon Poetry altogether — I leave the higher & deeper Kinds to Wordsworth, the delightful, popular & simply dignified to Southey; & reserve for myself the honorable attempt to make others feel and understand their writings, as they deserve to be felt and understood."[2] Coleridge failed to finish "Christabel," which was to be the "Ancient Mariner" of the second volume, and contributed only one new poem, a Gothic confection called "Love" that they inserted into the sequence of the first volume. The second volume, then, became entirely Wordsworth's showcase. For the original *Lyrical Ballads* the poets preferred anonymity because, as Coleridge put it, "Wordsworth's name is nothing" and "to a large number of persons mine *stinks*."[3] The greatly expanded, two-volume edition of 1800 appeared actually in January of 1801, and, with Coleridge's blessing, under the authority of Wordsworth's name alone.

Wordsworth had published separately two longish poems in 1793 — *An Evening Walk* and *Descriptive Sketches* — that, despite some strong passages, seem on the whole to be trapped in just the kind of eighteenth-century hokeyness he would disparage in his famous preface to *Lyrical Ballads*. These received scant attention from critics and readers, although Coleridge noticed them. The 1800 *Lyrical Ballads*, then, is Wordsworth's first significant publication under his own name. This fact, along with the occasionally tedious, frequently pompous, overtly defensive but nonetheless influential preface, which Coleridge claimed in a letter to Southey as "half a child of my own Brain" fifteen years before denouncing it publicly in the *Biographia*, confirms Wordsworth's ambition to assert himself as a professional author — and as an innovative poet with ideas for correcting all that has gone wrong with poetry in the final quarter of the eighteenth century. These claims are familiar to English majors and probably to most creative writers, and summaries of Wordsworth's most important points are to be found easily enough. For my purposes here, the most important thing to keep in mind is that, in the 1800 *Lyrical Ballads*, Wordsworth is introducing himself to the poetry-reading public with an obstreperous *braggadocio* that, of course, masks the insecurity of an author who is conscious of a readership that may not care about or understand what he is trying to do.

In the simple "Advertisement" that opens the 1798 *Lyrical Ballads* Wordsworth had hoped to counter his readers' "preestablished codes of decision"; now, in the first draft of the Preface to *Lyrical Ballads*, he is doing battle openly with a public whose taste he regards as "depraved," involving a "degrading thirst after outrageous stimulation" in a popular culture that he variously describes as "gaudy," "inane," "sickly," "stupid," "idle," "extravagant," "false," "curiously elaborate," and essentially unnatural and inhuman.[4] While perhaps not rhetorically astute in his evident hostility towards his own readers, Wordsworth is here frustrated by a culture that seems too interested in cheap thrills and shallow sentimentality instead of deep thought and powerful feeling. And he's worried about the survival of his work in such a climate. The Preface, by which Wordsworth hoped to justify himself, had mixed success at first, although the book would go through two more editions by 1805. It was for many years Wordsworth's only title to demand a printing beyond the first.

Many of the new poems in the 1800 *Lyrical Ballads* are darker (thanks to Goslar) and concern themselves, like "There Was a Boy," with mortality and ephemerality—and, less frequently, their opposites. The second edition shows Wordsworth experimenting more with lyric. It includes the two groups of poems popularly known as the Matthew poems and the Lucy poems but sometimes also referred to as the "Goslar lyrics." There, Wordsworth also began experimenting with short lyrics, producing some of the strangest, most psychologically probing poems of his career. These dark poems explore the isolation of subjectivity: the mysterious Lucy poems do so in relation generally to quasi-erotic themes, while the poignant Matthew poems juxtapose youth with old age through layers of recollection. In the latter set, "The Fountain" and "The Two April Mornings," Wordsworth develops a composite character based on his Hawkshead schoolmaster, Reverend William Taylor, and on an old storytelling peddler who would visit the school—the same peddler who inspired the Pedlar character Wordsworth would continue to develop for "The Recluse," and who eventually became the Wanderer of *The Excursion*. Matthew is an elderly schoolteacher, nature-lover, father-figure, playmate, and rustic poet. Among the poems Wordsworth wrote about Matthew in Goslar is a series of five elegies that lament his passing. Remembering Matthew, Wordsworth writes, "I feel more sorrow in a smile / Than in a waggon-load of tears." Wordsworth's speaker admonishes his now-adult fellow schoolmates, "Both in your sorrow and your bliss / Remember him and his grey head."[5] In Goslar, Wordsworth develops the complicated, paradoxical attitude of grief that marks much of his writing about death.

In "The Fountain" and "The Two April Mornings" Matthew comes to life as Wordsworth develops conversation between Matthew and his young companion framed by the recollection of the adult speaker who had been that boy — now-and-then projections of Wordsworth himself. The Matthew poems present the speaker in relation to his past just as the remembered dialogues present his younger self in conversation with the much older man. These are subtle poems about loss and mortality, made even more so by the recognizable distance between the speaker of the poem and the boy who talks with Matthew, even though they are the same person. In "The Two April Mornings," the spring day reminds Matthew of a previous day that reminded him of the pain of his daughter's death — "Yon cloud with that long purple cleft / Brings fresh into my mind / A day like this which I have left / Full thirty years behind." Thirty years ago, Matthew explains, he stopped at the grave of his daughter, who already had been dead for nine years, and spotted a young girl who reminds him of his loss. He says, "There came from me a sigh of pain / Which I could ill confine; / I looked at her and looked again; / — And did not wish her mine." His pain is complicated by the comparison between the living and the dead girls and the awareness that this other young girl could never replace his own daughter. If the April morning — with all of its associations of rebirth — is the site for revelations of mortality and loss, we realize by the end that there are, in a sense, three April mornings: the one that reminds Matthew of his loss, the one Matthew describes, and finally the present moment of recollection and composition that both recalls and engenders the supposed memory and poetic image of Matthew "with his bough /

Of wilding in his hand" with which the poem ends. Now "in his grave," Matthew is recalled in abstraction, emphasizing how utterly the corporeal man, like his daughter, no longer exists.[6] Here, memory is not palliative when it reminds one of change and loss. But the literary character persists. Wordsworth fictionalizes everything, so that the adult speaker, the boy companion, and even the old man are creative composites, imaginative projections of Wordsworth himself more than they are actual memories — even though they might be based on experience.

Both sets of poems involve the death of a young girl. More so than most of Wordsworth's other short lyrics, the Lucy poems in particular are mysterious mini-symbolist masterpieces in their sparse but suggestive language, intense imagery, and psychological depth. The death of Lucy, like the death of Matthew's daughter, is more likely an expression of angst regarding Wordsworth's feelings towards his unknown daughter than, as Coleridge supposed, his fear of losing his sister. Like Matthew, Lucy is probably a composite of people Wordsworth knew — or, poignantly, some kind of projection of the poet's guilt in relation to his unknown daughter, here given a name of both English and French derivation from Latin. These poems are as obliquely suggestive — and as morbid — as later poems by Poe or Dickinson. Recognizing their contemporaneity with the autobiographical thinking and writing Wordsworth was doing in Goslar is provocative; if they belong to Wordsworth's other writing of the poet's self, they remain uncharacteristically indeterminate — and satisfyingly so.

The most magnificent of these Goslar lyrics, "A Slumber Did My Spirit Seal," may be the most commented-upon eight lines in all of English literature, beginning with Coleridge's proclamation of it as a "sublime Epitaph."[7] Coleridge is being cannily oxymoronic since sublime suggests greatness or magnitude, while an epitaph usually is short enough to fit on a headstone. Although considered one of the Lucy poems, this one gives no name to the departed and begs the question of whether the poem is even about the death of a person:

A slumber did my spirit seal,
　I had no human fears:
She seem'd a thing that could not feel
　The touch of earthly years.

No motion has she now, no force;
　She neither hears nor sees;
Roll'd round in earth's diurnal course
　With rocks and stones and trees![8]

The greatness of the poem is its inscrutability. Wordsworth suggests plenty but does not directly reveal much: the distinction of there being "a slumber" implies right away that the slumber is death and that maybe the grieving speaker euphemistically calls it a "slumber" because he is still coming to terms with the reality of death. Curiously, though, the word "spirit" does not explicitly belong to the deceased but to the speaker—"my spirit." This death has closed up his "spirit"—but how? By ending his happiness? By closing him off from others now that he has lost his loved one? Or does it mean to seal as in to stamp or to make an impression upon something? This "slumber" has somehow marked his "spirit"?

Is this a rare Wordsworthian love poem? The gendering of the spirit as female yet possessed by a presumably masculine subjectivity (the "my" and "I" pronouns) suggests that it might be a poem about how an all-consuming erotic desire for the loved object has failed to acknowledge her humanity. Perhaps this recognition, as much as the loss itself, results in a profound marking or delimiting of the speaker's "spirit." Clearly, this slumber has exposed his naivety and the profound limitations of his desire for her to stay the same. In the final stanza, the speaker does seem to accept the reality of death but does so in language that is either starkly obvious or bitterly ironic: "No motion has she now, no force; / She neither hears nor sees." These lines are ironic because they seem to be the literal realization of what previously had precluded his "human fears" — that the "spirit," gendered female, was not human, not mortal, and thus not alive. The stark imagery of the conclusion perhaps suggests a becoming one again with nature — from "dust to dust", as in Genesis 3:19. Although this is a natural consolation, the final lines also point back to the designation of her as "a thing" while alive, and we may find it somewhat disturbing that the poem ends with his delusion of her inhumanity confirmed. Again, the living spirit is an unknowable impossibility. Has she achieved immortality as part of the dynamic generative cycle of life — "earth's diurnal course" — or merely achieved the static condition — "a thing that could not feel" — imposed upon her while she was alive?

But what if this poem does not even belong among the Lucy poems, which were assembled as such by Matthew Arnold long after Wordsworth's death? It may be a dark reminder of the psychological isolation a lover feels, even in intimate connection to another person. But what if it is also about memory, creativity, and writing? Instead of being one of the Lucy poems, "A Slumber Did My Spirit Seal," contemporaneous as its composition is with Wordsworth's earliest writing for *The Prelude*, may also be quasi-autobiographical meta-writing about the epic project underway. The anxieties and ambiguities I have interpreted above could stand just as well as figurations of Wordsworth's experience of putting ideas into words, vocalizing them, only to have them fixed on paper in script and then print, finally bound as books. The psychological and ontological distress the poem suggests is a symbolic expression of Wordsworth's extreme aversion to publishing his works—even as his literary ambitions and financial concerns necessitated his doing so. In March of 1798, Wordsworth described publication as "a thing which I dread as much as death itself."[9] Shortly after his return to England, Wordsworth expressed this antipathy to none other than his publisher as he awaited the reviews of *Lyrical Ballads*: "My aversion from publication," Wordsworth writes, "increases every day, so much so, that no motives whatever, nothing but pecuniary necessity, will, I think, ever prevail upon me to commit myself to the press again."[10] His sister later remarked that Wordsworth would "leave all his works to be published after his Death" if he did not need the modest income he received from their sales.[11]

Wordsworth equated the fixing of his poetry on paper to death and interment and preferred to describe the making of poems as "composition" rather than as "writing." Remarking on Wordsworth's perception of publication as "the exhaustion of artistic vitality," Duncan Wu cites a striking simile from *The Prelude*—itself part of a larger epic simile— in which the poet explains the stultifying effect of urban life on imaginative perception: his senses battered and benumbed, the city dweller's perception of the scene before him appears as "Exposed and lifeless as a written book."[12] As befits this neo-Neo-Platonist, Wordsworth considered publication to be a kind of slumber, then, that seals the creative spirit by delimiting it, leaving only a textual monument behind—an epitaph. That "sublime epitaph," "A Slumber Did My Spirit Seal," concludes with the spirit "rolled round," encased even, with "rocks and stones and trees." As surprising as this view of books may be to bibliophiles, Wordsworth nonetheless worries that books are as ephemeral as mortality, profoundly unsatisfactory as a means of preserving spirit. But anyone who's ever lost a hard drive will know what he means.

This concern is profoundly relevant to Wordsworth's ontological adaptation of his memories as part of making a writerly self. A writer figuratively seeks immortality, right? But what if the medium for preserving the writerly self is itself mortal? In Book Five of the thirteen-book version of *The Prelude,* called significantly "Books," Wordsworth employs a stone and a shell as symbols for two kinds of books (mathematics and poetry) as part of a peculiar *non sequitur* interrupting the narrative of his Cambridge education. Wordsworth laments the perishability of those vessels "worthy of unconquerable life" in the eventual obviation of them by spiritual immortality or in the apocalyptic destruction of the earth. What will become of our books?

> But all the meditations of mankind,
> Yea, all the adamantine holds of truth,
> By reason built, or passion, which itself
> Is highest reason in a soul sublime;
> The consecrated works of Bard and Sage,
> Sensuous or intellectual, wrought by men,
> Twin labourers and heirs of the same hopes,
> Where would they be? Oh! why hath not the mind
> Some element to stamp her image on
> In nature somewhat nearer to her own?
> Why, gifted with such powers to send abroad
> Her spirit, must it lodge in shrines so frail?[13]

In these rather grandiose terms, Wordsworth expresses not only his concern for the permanence of the written word but also his frustration with it as a means of representing the mind; the mind, moreover, is gendered female like the spirit sealed by slumber, and its intellectual spirit lodged not in the frail shrine of corporeal humanity but in language, text, and material artifact—all subject to decay. This explains why Wordsworth, a Frankenstein-like compositor of the parts of his own body of work, obsessively revised and reprinted his poems as if emendation were reanimation, a means of keeping them—and himself—alive.

This fifth book, "Books," which opens with the anxiety of the ephemerality of books, builds to a rumination on poetry, that sublime intellectual power mortified in print and on paper — textual incarnation. Closing a circle, Wordsworth recalls the metaphor of the breeze from the "glad preamble" to celebrate the Wordsworthian article of faith that "he, who, in his youth / A wanderer among the woods and fields, / With living Nature hath been intimate," will also, by virtue of that training, "receive enduring touches of deep joy / From the great Nature that exists in works / Of mighty poets." He makes explicit the connection between the "corresponding mild creative breeze" and "the mystery of words":

> Visionary Power
> Attends the motions of the viewless winds
> Embodied in the mystery of words:
> There darkness makes abode, and all the host
> Of shadowy things work endless changes there,
> As in a mansion like their proper home.
> Even forms and substances are circumfused
> By that transparent veil with light divine;
> And, through the turnings intricate of verse,
> Present themselves as objects recognized,
> In flashes, and with glory not their own.[14]

If only Shelley had lived to read those words he might have been reconciled with the poetic father he believed to have forsaken him.[15] It is the secret rites of words — not in the books, those "shrines so frail" — that ideas, like Platonic forms, find "their proper home," a mystical intercourse between signified and signifier. Ultimately, this is all a metaphor for reading, for the fact that a similar intercourse between writer and reader happens also in the "mansion" of the mind. As he says to Dorothy in "Tintern Abbey," her experiences will become memories, "when thy mind / Shall be a mansion for all lovely forms."[16] Wordsworth sounds like Plato — except he prefers poetry in all of its mad artifice and its emotionally provocative propensities. Those "turnings intricate of verse," which sound like the very qualities Wordsworth famously criticizes in the Preface to *Lyrical Ballads,* are part of the mystery in making ideas we know to be true all of a sudden fresh and revivified. This is what we want poetry to do — to reinvigorate the shared humanity in us. To remind us, as Wordsworth says in "The Old Cumberland Beggar," "That we have all of us one human heart."[17]

And now for an anticlimax. At one stage of composition, in 1804, *The Prelude* ends here — except that Wordsworth adds an apology for providing such "a scanty record . . . Of what I owed to Books in early life."[18] Wordsworth did draft, however, a slightly different conclusion to the fifth book, the final book in this version of *The Prelude,* one that differs from the thirteen-book version in acknowledging Wordsworth's reader's particular interest. In the thirteen-book version, Wordsworth closes the chapter by explaining why his tribute to books and reading appears at this point in his narrative. He writes that,

> . . . as this work was taking in my thoughts
> Proportions that seemed larger than had first
> Been meditated, I was indisposed
> To any further progress at a time
> When these acknowledgements were left unpaid.[19]

Here is a recognition that this work, *The Prelude* to Coleridge, on his own life, is ever expanding in the poet's conception of it. However, Wordsworth strikes a different tone in a version Dorothy transcribed for Coleridge to take to Malta, where he intended to recover from his various addictions — uh, I mean, *ailments.* Wordsworth implicitly apologizes to his friend for the lack of progress on their project "The Recluse." He explains that "this meditative History / Was call-

ing me to a far different work / Which lies before us, yet
untouch'd," adding that since he was commenting upon "an
abasement" of his mind caused in part by "Books ill-chosen"
he "was loth to think / Of such ungracious office, at a time /
When these acknowledgments were yet unpaid."[20] Perhaps
there is a touch of passive-aggressive hostility in this ironic
deference to Coleridge's great intellect and wide reading.
(He had just been discussing his boyhood love for the *Arabian Nights* and other fantasy stories — as if Coleridge had
been reared, instead, on Berkeley and Hume.) This speaks
volumes about the dynamic between the two men: Wordsworth is apologizing for not having been shaped by the
powerful intellectual forces that made Coleridge the most
brilliant thinker in England, while also alluding to their
shared project, "Which lies before us, yet untouch'd," and
slyly reproving his friend for putting the weight of that task
on his shoulders alone.

That work remained mostly "untouch'd." When he realized "The Recluse" would never be written, Wordsworth
could not face the publication of his autobiographical poem,
which he had construed as a metonym for his ability to write
the "philosophical Poem, containing views of Man, Nature,
and Society."[21] Publication would have been the outing of
his great professional failure. Although he never did write
"The Recluse," Wordsworth for many years continued to
make a lot of noise about getting ready to do it. This year
will be the year, he would announce annually. All the while
Wordsworth, a Shandean figure, but tragic rather than
comic, failed to realize that he had already written the great
epic of his time. Instead, Wordsworth left behind this lowering project, "The Recluse," that he could never finish — and a
big part of it, *The Excursion*, which Byron, Shelley, and nearly
everyone else (except, curiously, Keats) deplored but which
the Victorians thought was his masterpiece. Thus Wordsworth consigned his actual masterpiece, *The Prelude*, to posterity as a monument of that epic failure.

But Wordsworth did finish *The Excursion* and with it he began conceiving of his oeuvre as being housed figuratively in "the body of a gothic Church," as we have already seen, to which *The Prelude* was to be its "Anti-chapel." "The Recluse" was to be the nave, presumably. Continuing the metaphor, Wordsworth adds that his other poems, "when they shall be properly arranged," will be like "the little Cells, Oratories, and sepulchral Recesses" of a gothic cathedral. Having already written the "Books" book of *The Prelude*, Wordsworth needed this figurative psychological fortification to "lodge" the images of his mind. But, again, "The Recluse" was a cathedral built in air, like Kubla Khan's pleasure-dome. He contented himself with writing hundreds of sonnets. As an old man in his sixties and seventies, finally becoming, reluctantly in 1843, Queen Victoria's Poet Laureate, Wordsworth oversaw multiple new multi-volume editions of his *Poetical Works* while always renovating more or less the interior. His final one appeared in 1849. He finally was resigned: Cloth, paper, and ink would have to do to contain his astonishingly prolific body of work.

The architecture of his Works was strong enough, but the 1850 publication of *The Prelude* is itself a rather frail shrine for housing Wordsworth's writing life / life writing. As several of Wordsworth's late twentieth- and early twenty-first-century editors acknowledge, we have no final, definitive version of the poem that we can be certain is the version Wordsworth authorized. Since the publication of the thirteen-book *Prelude* by Ernest de Selincourt in 1926, scholars have debated the virtues of that earlier version against those of the fourteen-book *Prelude*, pitting the Wordsworth of the great decade (1798–1807) when he wrote his best loved poems against the older Wordsworth whose poetry is read now only by specialists. In 1974 Jonathan Wordsworth and Stephen Gill published the two-part *Prelude* of 1799, which they first presented as a standalone work. Since then, Duncan Wu has conjectured a five-book *Prelude* of 1804 that is, too, he asserts, an independent work with its own merits; and Jonathan Wordsworth has argued that the Goslar notebook can be made into a coherent poem of 1798 that he calls "Was It for This?"[22] Moreover, the vagaries of some of the emendations preserved in the 1850 book have cast doubt on the authority of those changes Wordsworth's executors made to the poem. Indeed, even the latest fair copy, made in 1839 while Wordsworth was still living, is of dubious authority, transcribed by the poet's daughter and her cousin. Wordsworth made some corrections but further emendations took place in April of 1850 in the days just after the poet's death.

In order to represent the fourteen-book *Prelude* (and thus distinguish the older Wordsworth's poem from the thirteen-book fair copy completed in 1806) editor W. J. B. Owen presents not the 1850 publication but a composite one, mostly based on the fair copy completed in 1839 but also informed by an assortment of manuscripts dating back to 1824. No wonder Wordsworth fretted over the ephemerality of books and obsessively revised and reorganized his other poetry. He left *The Prelude* for us to sort out, presuming we would read the 1839 one but preserving the earlier ones nonetheless, and was unconcerned that we might have difficulty doing so. What did he care? He was going to be dead anyway. He figured that *The Excursion*, his great Ode, and especially his five hundred sonnets, including such classics as *Ecclesiastical Sketches* and *Sonnets upon the Punishment of Death*, would memorialize him well enough.

spots of Time

There are in our existence spots of time
Which with distinct pre-eminence retain
A fructifying virtue, whence, depressed
By trivial occupations and the round
Of ordinary intercourse, our minds
(Especially the imaginative power)
Are nourished, and invisibly repaired.
Such moments chiefly seem to have their date
In our first childhood.[1]

William Blake should have read *The Prelude* instead of *The Excursion*, which gave him a bowel complaint.[2] But, like almost everyone else, he didn't know it existed. Had he been able to read *The Prelude*, he would have appreciated Wordsworth's grappling with the competing claims of rationalism and empiricism, with results that might have pleased the great visionary. He still would have argued with him about the relationship between imagination and memory. Wordsworth accepts transcendental knowledge in the sense that the mind is capable of *a priori* knowledge, or knowledge independent of experience. Wordsworth attributes this knowledge to Nature, the "efficacious spirit" that convinces him that "the mind / Is lord and master."[3] But the knowing still happens in the mind: what is outside of the mind re-minds the poet of what is in the mind. It sounds like rationalism in the preeminence of the intellect, but it has a mystical relationship to Nature that *The Prelude* explores without attempting to systematize a method. Wordsworth is not interested in reasoning through this aspect of his experience. It is all about creativity, which is Wordsworth's trademark.

The title of the 1805 version of Book Eleven of *The Prelude*

(Book Twelve in 1850) is "Imagination, How Impaired and Restored." As I have already suggested, much of what seems in Wordsworth to be philosophical rumination is actually his working out a poetics to explain himself and the writing of himself / his self. In his writing about the imagination, Wordsworth often sounds like an early Transcendentalist—and certainly he influenced them (Emerson called on Wordsworth at home but left disappointed—you should never meet your heroes). Typically, Wordsworth uses what we take to be transcendental as a conceivable metaphor for what is actually taking place inside, not outside, the mind, as he sees it. The spirit is "*in* the woods," not outside of it.[4] It is also in *him* and nowhere else. It's all an act of the imagination—even the parts of it that seem to be remembered. In Book Eleven of the 1805 version, Wordsworth writes of recovering from an over-confidence in empiricism, the "tyranny" of the five senses:

> I had felt
> Too forcibly, too early in my life,
> Visitings of imaginative power
> For this to last: I shook the habit off
> Entirely and for ever, and again
> In Nature's presence stood, as I stand now,
> A sensitive, and a creative soul.[5]

Yet, just as we might expect an explanation of "how" the imagination was "restored," after reading hundreds of lines about "how" it was "impaired," Wordsworth shrugs it off— the crisis simply passed. While his explanation may seem jejune, we find ourselves comfortable in the inevitability of the resolution: the then-self stood in "Nature's presence," as the now-self does now, as a "A sensitive and a creative soul." In other words, at this moment, those distinct beings, "myself" and "some other being," are both poets. His point is that his upbringing by nature, described throughout *The*

Prelude, has fortified his mind, his imagination, and his heart against such temporary crises. And again we might wonder how "The Recluse" could have done its work any better than this.

Because he is a poet and not a metaphysician, Wordsworth must translate whatever the mind can do with experience into words, into poetic form, even though it can never do justice; Wordsworth, most of the time, believes that the medium of poetry can create in his reader's mind an image approximate to what in the poet's mind inspired the verse. Sometimes he doubts it, shortly after he presents the sight of a "snow-white Ram" and its reflection in the water in Book IX of *The Excursion*:

> —Ah! that such beauty, varying in the light
> Of living nature, cannot be pourtrayed
> By words, nor by the pencil's silent skill;
> But is the property of him alone
> Who hath beheld it, noted it with care,
> And in his mind recorded it with love![6]

Wordsworth here thinks of the limitations of language and of writing more as a propriety that respects the privacy of perception and a discretion that can only politely suggest the goings-on of the mind, memory and imagination.

Like Blake, Wordsworth and Coleridge wanted to rehabilitate the imagination after its denigration in the seventeenth century by thinkers such as Descartes and Hobbes, who both considered it inferior to reason, and after the relative lack of interest in it during most of the eighteenth century. Like Kant, Fichte, and Schelling, they were interested in the relationship between memory and, more ostensibly, creative functions of the mind, between the reproductive and productive imaginations. Coleridge rejected empiricism because its methodology implies a too passive mind. He writes to Tom Poole that for someone like Newton

"*Mind* in his system is always passive — a lazy looker-on in an external world." Obviously empiricism cannot account for aesthetic or idealistic habits of mind. Kant's "disinterestedness" or objective aesthetic has something to do with an empirical approach. But it cannot account for something like "the sense of beauty." Coleridge goes on: "If the mind be not *passive*, if it be indeed made in God's image, & that too in the sublimest sense — the Image of the *Creator* — there is ground for suspicion that any system built on the passiveness of the mind must be false, as a system."[7]

From this perspective on creativity, the static "I am" ought not to mean "I am being" or "I have become"; it always means the more active "I am becoming" under the guise of saying "I was" or "I was becoming." Becoming never fully becomes being, if that makes any sense. "I was" is even weirder. The state of being retrospectively represented as "having been" or as "was" in the creative imagination — if that is what Wordsworth is doing — is similar to what Coleridge calls the "repetition in the finite mind of the eternal act of creation in the infinite I AM," or the "primary imagination." The "secondary imagination," according to Coleridge, is then the deliberate exertion of the same kind of creative agency, "differing only in degree, and in the mode of its operation." The creative imagination that makes art, thus, essentially "re-creates" Creation itself by imitating in the finite mind what God has done and presumably continues to do. Coleridge puns on the Biblical Hebrew *Yahweh*, which means "I am," and alludes to the *Ich bin* that pervades his reading in Kant, Fichte, and Schelling and their inquiries into subjectivity.[8] Although the mortal mind may be finite, as Coleridge writes, the repetition has infinite potential at least for creativity as long as the creative mind is capable of accessing it.

Wordsworth never sounds as abstract in his remarks on creativity and the imagination as Coleridge does, but his thinking about the topic is similar and was influenced by

Coleridge—as the preface to his 1815 collected *Poems* attests. There, Wordsworth scoops his former collaborator by putting into print his own explanation of Coleridge's ideas about the imagination and fancy two years before Coleridge would do. Both poets are interested in the relationship between imagination and memory and agree that "fancy," formerly synonymous with "memory," is a lesser power that involves simply the reorganization of images pulled from memory.[9] It is not, strictly speaking, creative. When he does write about the creative imagination Wordsworth employs terminology more applicable to the poet's work of making something out of it. In 1802, he wrote that the poet's job is to refine the feelings of his readers, to paint deeper shades in their responses to the world around them—essentially, as he writes, to "render their feeling more sane pure and permanent, that is, to eternal nature, and the great moving spirit of things."[10] This is, I think, what is implied in Coleridge's definitions of the primary and secondary imaginations. Wordsworth sees the task of "a great Poet" as teaching others how to appreciate the creativity in their own experience, of, as he writes in "Tintern Abbey," "all the mighty world / Of eye and ear, both what they half-create, / And what perceive."[11] This is partly Lockean empiricism, partly something else. It is close to Blake's aphorism "As a man is, so he sees." But where Blake creates one hundred percent of everything he sees, Wordsworth sees perception more as a fifty-fifty proposition.

If perception is half invention then how much of memory is imagined, created from the remnants of experience? More than half, certainly. Wordsworth admits as much in his conception of "spots of time," which he defines as particularly impressive moments from the past that are colored in one's memory by an awareness of the mind's sublime power and that "retain / A renovating Virtue." Much as he does in "Tintern Abbey," Wordsworth explains that memory has the power to restore, to repair, and to renovate one's spirit; but here he places less emphasis on Nature's role in this process and more on the mind's internal activity:

> This efficacious spirit chiefly lurks
> Among those passages of life in which
> We have had deepest feeling that the mind
> Is lord and master, and that outward sense
> Is but the obedient servant of her will.[12]

Since this passage comes near the end of *The Prelude*, it comes in the context of a resolution to the problems developed up to this point: after suffering what he considers to be an impairment of his mind, he realizes that his memories have helped him to recover the imaginative power he frequently demonstrates in his other poetry—particularly in poems such as "Tintern Abbey" or "I Wandered Lonely as a Cloud." But *The Prelude* is about how he gained that power, how he nearly lost it, and how he fully recovered it to become the poet he has been since then.

After the crisis, he finds himself revitalized in having arrived at self-fulfillment. He has become The Poet. *The Prelude*, then, is a poetic version of the *Künstlerroman*, or novel about the artist's growth from childhood to recognition of the protagonist's calling and realization of his talent. Since Wordsworth's poetry contains moments of intense perceptions that are peculiar to him, his task, as he moves towards the climax of *The Prelude* in Book Thirteen (1805), is to convey those experiences and insights so that the reader may experience the pleasure and, hopefully, the moral benefit of them.

The big difference between the two-part *Prelude* and the longer thirteen- and fourteen-book versions is Wordsworth's sense of having a public purpose, what he describes as a lifting of "The Being into magnanimity."[13] Whereas Book Eleven shows Wordsworth's imagination restored in relation to nature, Book Twelve must complete the project by doing so in relation to humankind. In this way, much of the conclusion of *The Prelude* reads like a mission statement for "The Recluse" and, at the same time, an article of surrender, admitting the impossibility of doing what Coleridge wanted him to do—that is, write the great philosophical epic that would change the world. Wordsworth hints at the sorts of material, "abstruser argument," he might cover in such a poem, any one of which would be "a worthy theme / For philosophic Verse." He dismisses them as "matter for another Song," however, because he has no place for any of those topics here.[14] He is back to where he was at the beginning of the thirteen- and fourteen-book *Prelude*, reviewing potential subjects for epic argument.

But he also has to build up to a conclusion, a big finish, a payoff. So he introduces the "spots of time" passage, which he wrote around the same time as the fragments in the Goslar notebook. In the thirteen- and fourteen-book versions, therefore, the placement of the passage has more to do with narrative structure than with developing a philosophical position. Wordsworth presents the "spots of time" passage in order to redress the tyranny of the senses over the mind. Wordsworth then provides two instances that demonstrate how the "spots of time" function and that exemplify "those passages of life in which / We have had deepest feeling that the mind / Is lord and master." These moments are also those when Wordsworth "seems" to comprise "two consciousnesses" most emphatically, one of them possibly the mind asserting itself as "lord and master." Or are there three consciousnesses? The third might be the mind itself, distinct from the other "two consciousnesses," acting as "lord and master" of them both.

Regardless, something important happens in the mind of the poet—most likely while writing the "spots of time" into being. In the first example, Wordsworth describes himself at the age of six riding across the hills with an adult servant from whom he becomes separated; he finds himself lost on the moor at the foot of a decaying gibbet where a

murderer long ago had been executed. He finds the name
of the murderer carved in "monumental writing." The image
likely inspired Dickens' description of Pip's fear in the opening chapter of *Great Expectations*, but Wordsworth does not
mention having been disturbed by it. The poet's juxtaposition of death, murder, and writing is psychologically suggestive. Mary Jacobus sees the poet inscribing his own poetic
immortality: "Wordsworth, in effect, carves his own name
in place of the murderer's, so that it may live for ever." As
Jacobus notes, the passage appears in the two-part *Prelude*
but without the inscription.[15] Wordsworth added that passage for the 1805 version, which is, as I have asserted, more
explicitly about being a writer. Weird projections of guilt
aside, the passage does seem to be self-reflexively obsessed
with words. As the boy leaves the gibbet, he sees a girl carry-
ing a pitcher on her head and struggling against the wind,
her garments billowing suggestively. But surprisingly, it is
this much less remarkable image that inspires his imagination: he says he would "need / Colours and words that
are unknown to man / To paint the visionary dreariness"
that pervades the scene but that nonetheless provides him
with the same kind of restorative memory that a more glorious scene, such as he describes in "Tintern Abbey," does.[16]
In language that resembles the end of Coleridge's "Kubla
Khan," he exclaims that, as memories come upon him "from
the dawn almost / Of life," he would "enshrine the spirit of
the past / For future restoration" — but only "as far as words
can give."[17] In this sense, perhaps, Wordsworth does write
his name over that of the murderer. But why? According to
Jacobus, referring to Paul de Man's work, "*The Prelude* reminds us that central to all autobiography is the longing for
invulnerability to death."[18] This suggestion has a Freudian
ring of truth in the passage that closes Book Eleven, which
involves the boy's excitement about returning home for
Christmas only to be orphaned by the death of his father
just a few days later. The important thing to remember is

that the concept of "spots of time" allows for creative ambiguity in the construction / reconstruction of memories as episodes. The "efficacious spirit" actually lurks in our "feeling," not our certainty, that the mind was controlling the episode of one's life — this, of course, is not happening then but in the moment of writing, which is when the mind is supremely powerful.

While the concept of "spots of time" is a metaphor for writing about oneself and one's memories, I see it also as a meta-figure for creativity and writing. Wordsworth found inspiration in what I have called elsewhere "formal para-doxy" — that is the yoking of disparate forms, sub-genres, and modes, with all their attendant readerly expectations, to make a nonce form.[19] The notion of a "lyrical ballad" is para-doxical, for instance: a lyric is a short, non-narrative poem of introspection that develops insights, ideas, or emotions (with classical origins); by contrast, a ballad is a long narrative poem that tells a story (with folk origins). In the Preface to *Lyrical Ballads* Wordsworth distinguishes "Goody Blake and Harry Gill" as exemplary because it is written in, or fashioned with, as he says, "a more impressive metre than is usual in Ballads."[20] The lyric is associated with virtuosity, that is, a virtuoso performance. In addition to all the traditional literary handbook definitions of lyric, I tend to think of a lyric moment as a particularly self-conscious formal performance: obviously, in the traditional sense, lyric need not only have a song-like quality but it does require the development of some insight, some feeling or idea. This is essential to the sonnet, which is, after all, a little song. And this distinguishes lyric from narrative — though narrative may contain lyric moments that disrupt or suspend narrative movement, providing an opportunity for the poet — the maker — to perform the making of the thing poets are supposed to make.

The two-book *Prelude* is a bit like a very long "Tintern Abbey." And, therefore, since it focuses on episodes and the effect of them on the then-self and the now-self, I would say it is more lyric than narrative. The longer, thirteen- and fourteen-book versions of *The Prelude* are more patently narrative, more autobiographically linear in the tracing of "the history of a Poet's mind" and replete with incidents that, ordered as they are, make a plot with sub-plots. The "spots of time" examples that Wordsworth moves to Book Eleven (Twelve) are already fixed as part of the poem in 1799. To expand the poem Wordsworth would have to come up with—er, recall—many more. But only these two moments are specifically tagged as such. In the longer versions, the "spots of time" and other similar moments of rumination in the poem appear as interpolated lyric moments in an overarching narrative. They are points at which the timbre of the verse changes to announce, "here comes some poetry!"

The very phrase "spots of time" encapsulates the tension between narrative and lyric. At the risk of sounding like I've been watching too much *Star Trek* and *Doctor Who*, a "spot of time" is a space-time paradox and, as a literary term, an oxymoron. This is how Wordsworth conceives of the formal paradoxy of *The Prelude*. Similarly, "spot" is a place, a locus of imaginative power, a lyric center of gravity; "of" signifies the relationship between a part and a whole; "time" is the larger narrative, the sequence of events. Because they are episodic, however, these moments, these "passages of life," suggest that they are also liminal, are movable. Thus, towards the end of *The Prelude*, we find a particularly recursive Wordsworth, who doesn't know how to end the poem because, chronologically, the best stuff has already happened. Wordsworth allows that the writing of one's life not only permits but invites such reconstruction, recreation, reordering. So, he violates the chronology of *The Prelude*, the narrative, to privilege the lyric, but, paradoxically, does so all in the service of narrative convention—beginning, middle, end. In other words, Wordsworth does not have a narrative climax for his poem (after all, he is still living his life, and publishing a moderately successful book that even some of

your friends disliked was not much of a high point); so, because he has become the poet of *The Prelude*, he has to demonstrate it by saving the best "spot of time" for last.

So, Wordsworth chooses revelation over catastrophe.
In order to make a satisfying climax to such a long poem,
Wordsworth found he had to twist the chronology of that
poem. The climactic moment of both self-actualization and
supreme poetic vision occurs at the end of the longer poem,
the thirteen- and fourteen-book versions, in the climbing of
Mount Snowdon. Book Twelve (1805), in 1850 Book Thirteen, concludes the restoration of Wordsworth's imagination and prepares the way for the final book; it also an-
nounces that he has found his theme, the lack of which he
had lamented at the beginning of *The Prelude*. The final spot
of time is his description of climbing Snowdon in Wales
with Robert Jones, the companion who crossed the Alps
with him the previous year. Significantly, the ascent of
Snowdon actually occurred in 1791, even as the work's timeline of events stops in 1798. Chronologically, then, the "spot
of time" shows Wordsworth becoming Wordsworth by 1791,
not by 1798, or possibly during the intervening five years between 1793 and 1798, as he suggests in "Tintern Abbey."

This reconstituting of self in a creative reorganization
of events is, as they say, poetic license. Wordsworth does
not misrepresent the timeline; he just twists it to pull what
happened in 1790 closer to the poet-person he is at the end
of *The Prelude*. The moment, the poetry of the moment, is
too good not to save for the end. The ascent of Snowdon in
the concluding book of *The Prelude* is everything that seeing
Mont Blanc is not. In Book Six, Wordsworth writes that he
and his companion:

> Beheld the summit of Mont Blanc, and grieved
> To have a soulless image on the eye,
> Which had usurp'd upon a living thought
> That never more could be. . . .[21]

It's not that the actual mountain is disappointing; it's just that the Mont Blanc Wordsworth had imagined previously, at least for the time being, had ceased to exist. And whatever attempts the imagination might make to recover that image, in effect, will adulterate it with visual imagery derived from the empirical event. Wordsworth adds that "the wondrous Vale / Of Chamouny" was sufficiently impressive but that the two mountaineers, in order to appreciate the sights, had to be "reconciled . . . to realities."[22] Significantly, the paragraph concludes in bathos with an uncharacteristic simile, comparing winter to a "tamed Lion."[23] The simile is, after all, the lamest, feeblest effort of the poetic imagination. I think Wordsworth intended the figurative anticlimax to underscore the disappointment of having the real Mont Blanc usurp the place of the imagined one.

The Mont Blanc episode is itself followed by the anticlimax of Wordsworth and Jones getting lost and finding out, to their further dismay, that they "had crossed the Alps" without knowing it. They retrace their steps and descend via the Simplon Pass into the Gondo ravine. But this event is prefaced by an apostrophe to "Imagination!" in which Wordsworth recognizes the "glory" of Imagination, not only in the experience—the "half" creating—but also in the remembering of it. The apostrophe, not connected specifically to any one location or experience, existing only in the context of crossing the Alps, shifts in time to the moment of writing, which occurred in 1804, where basically, in recalling and thus creating, Wordsworth is "blinded" by what Geoffrey Hartman describes as the "the independence of imagination from nature."[24] Wordsworth writes that he "was lost" and is in the moment of composition only "now recovering" by the use of his imagination. A reverse "usurpation," a foreshadowing of the poet's combating of the "tyranny" of the five senses, then takes place "when the light of sense / Goes out in flashes that have shewn to us / The invisible world." The paradox is fittingly a challenge to the imagination—

the light of sense goes dark in flashes of what can only be imagined (perhaps adapted from Milton's great oxymoron "darkness visible"). It is in the creative imagining of one's self, the reconfiguring of memory in a writerly moment, that, according to Wordsworth, "doth Greatness make abode" and convinces us, if only in our respective imaginations, that "Our destiny, our nature, and our home, / Is with infinitude." He adds that imagination gives hope of "something evermore about to be."[25]

According to the narrative logic of the "history of a Poet's mind," this recovery can happen in 1804 while writing about 1790 because of what happened atop Snowdon, or so the poet deduces in the final book, in the following year. So, the ascent of Snowdon does follow the crossing of the Alps, as it did in the poet's life; but, in *The Prelude*, it comes, not in the approximate space of nine months, or, say, in the next section of the poem, but after several thousand lines, which is a disproportionately longer span of time in terms of reading. But thus is the efficacy of the spots of time poetic: it imitates the way memory itself does not follow chronological order and provides an exquisitely beautiful conclusion to the poem that defies paraphrase and exegesis.

I have to admit that the writing of this last chapter is, for me — albeit on a much smaller scale — something like the prospect of writing "The Recluse" was for Wordsworth. The necessity of explaining what the ascent of Snowdon has to do with the making of a writerly self out of memories was a burden that turned out to be not as cumbersome as the anticipation of having to carry it. The conclusion of *The Prelude* is frequently excerpted in anthologies and justly so due to the power of the poetry; but it is also all the better, like all conclusions, for having the weight of what precedes it. Moreover, I do not want to "usurp" the experience by providing you with a gloss on what happens there. Suffice it to say that Wordsworth has a remarkable experience when he gets to the top. It is night and, in lines echoing Book Seven

of *Paradise Lost,* in which Milton describes Creation, Wordsworth writes that he found himself "on the shore . . . of a
huge sea of mist."[26] It is, as we might say crudely, a religious
experience. But it is an experience in which not one's soul
per se but one's mind feels "exalted by an underpresence, /
The sense of God, or whatso'er is dim / Or vast in its own
being."[27] This is familiar Wordsworth but better. Here is also
Wordsworth's most important statement of creativity, of
imagination, of poetry, and, indeed, nature / "Nature." And
it happens *after* the sublime spectacle he describes so per-
fectly. Then he introduces this most important statement:

> A meditation rose in me that night
> Upon the lonely Mountain when the scene
> Had pass'd away, and it appear'd to me
> The perfect image of a mighty Mind,
> Of one that feeds upon infinity. . . .

The older Wordsworth extensively revised these lines and
those that follow for the fourteen-book *Prelude,* downplay-
ing the mysticism, deism, or paganism possibly evoked by
them, adding more Milton to them, but not making them
more religious, just not as overtly not religious. For the
fourteen-book version he also clarifies that what is now "the
emblem of a Mind / That feeds upon infinity" refers to
the experience of seeing/imagining a sea of clouds at his
feet while atop the summit.[28] But I prefer the reading in
which the "it" that "appear'd to be "The perfect image of a
mighty Mind" refers to the "meditation" Wordsworth had
that night instead of or in addition to the "scene" (the par-
allelism of the syntax would actually point to the "meditation" as antecedent) because the mind, not the scene, is
really what is working here. The scene — significant word
choice — is activated by the mind, and of course this is all
happening now anyway, not then (the writer's now, the
reader's now).

Wordsworthian "Nature" finally is a "handmaid to a no-
bler [love] than herself" — in "second place," he writes, to
having fostered a more powerful and more important love
for humankind.[29] But the poet is still the preeminent exem-
plar of humankind because he can do for others what "Nature" has done for him. Ultimately, one imagines, Wordsworth must have believed that each of us could become like
this — or what would be the point? This is not an exercise in
self-aggrandizement. He is hoping that you will want to follow his example beginning with his precepts but developing
your own practice. I resist interpreting more of the conclusion and, instead, encourage you to read it. And here's why
you should: there is much to do here with life, love, and
imagination, which Wordsworth consummately calls "reason in her most exalted mood,"[30] which leads to a rumination on Wordsworth's own character and capacity for love.
He goes on to assert that the individual must "fashion" the
ability to combine imagination and "intellectual love" on
his or her own without anyone else's help — "No secondary hand can intervene" — and thus humankind may aspire
towards perfection.[31]

Finally, in tribute to Coleridge, Wordsworth looks forward to how valuable the work, the writing of these two
"joint-laborers" who are also "Prophets of Nature" will be
to future generations. Their ministry, not so "severe" perhaps as that which made Wordsworth, will be to "Instruct
them [future generations] how the mind of man becomes /
A thousand times more beautiful than the earth / On which
he dwells." "Becomes" — there it is again. And the last word,
in both the thirteen- and fourteen-book versions, is "divine."
The earth, green "Nature" (including daffodils), the "Frame
of things" (there's that word again), finally does not become
anything; it is already "divine." It is the mind that "is itself /
Of substance and of fabric more divine."[32] The writing of
one's self, the creative act of making that self, is superhuman
and that is why we do it.

Perhaps then the writer worships a god that dwells within himself, a god of his or her own making that entrusts the self with its idolatry in the things that he or she makes. But that making never ends and so the worship is itself an act of making.

Finale

Therefore, although it be a history
Homely and rude, I will relate the same
For the delight of a few natural hearts,
And with yet fonder feeling, for the sake
Of youthful Poets, who among these Hills
Will be my second Self when I am gone.[1]

The *Prelude* takes for granted that reading and writing are important life-affirming, mind-altering, soul-making activities. If this is true, then the poet — the writer — is quite possibly the most important person in the world. *The Prelude* is a poem about its author needing to believe he is necessary by convincing himself. But it is not a vanity project. Rather, it is an honest expression of what all artists must believe about themselves. The artist's chief mechanism of defense is to blame the public for its degraded sensibility and taste — or to deplore the forsaking of its very soul. As Wordsworth wrote to Lady Beaumont, one of his few admirers in 1807:

> It is an awful truth, that there neither is, nor can be, any genuine enjoyment of Poetry among nineteen out of twenty of those persons who live, or wish to live, in the broad light of the world — among those who either are, or are striving to make themselves, people of consideration in society. This is a truth, and an awful one, because to be incapable of a feeling of Poetry in my sense of the word is to be without love of human nature and reverence for God.[2]

This partly explains how and why Wordsworth could write and revise nine thousand lines of iambic pentameter about the development of his mind, his imagination, his very soul and then insist that it be published only after his death. Still, the work of writing one's self can never rest for a vitally creative person; and this explains why Wordsworth obsessively expanded, revised, and tinkered with the poem for nearly fifty years, instructing his executors to publish it once he could no longer be embarrassed by it.

Conversely, can Wordsworth explore the revelation of his poetic self without seeming too into himself? Can any writer attempt such a feat without redounding charges of egotism on himself/herself? The young Keats, who did not live long enough to read *The Prelude*, still recognized enough of Wordsworth's self in his other poetry to invent the phrase "egotistical sublime" as a way of describing that which is "wordsworthian" (Keats, in this letter, tellingly resists capitalizing the eponymous modifier).[3] Wordsworth, no more a narcissist or egotist than any other writer, was not completely comfortable with the making of either his former or his present self into the hero of a subjective, introspective epic poem. But Keats's phrase is easily misunderstood: Keats does not mean that Wordsworth's poetry is vain, swaggering, or conceited — although some of Wordsworth's other readers thought so. The *Oxford English Dictionary* explains that *egotism* involves "the practice of talking about oneself or one's doings." The point is that Wordsworth's personality impresses itself so strongly on the poetry that it has (or means to have) the aesthetic effect of the sublime. But it is not that Wordsworth thinks he is himself that awesome; it is that he is amazed to find what he finds inside of himself, amazed by what was put there for him to use. In his book for the Muse Books series on Blake and creativity, Eric G. Wilson writes that "the great problem for all who wish to create" is "how to transcend a past, both personal and cultural, that has shaped one's habits of perception."[4] This is not a problem for Wordsworth: the problem for him is that someone like Wilson, or like Keats, thinks he *should* transcend his past and its influence on him.

Wordsworth was worried that some readers would find his life-writing too self-indulgent, too idiosyncratic to matter. As James Dickey commented in a 1976 interview with *The Paris Review*, the problem with "confessional" or autobiographical poets such as Robert Lowell, Anne Sexton, or Sylvia Plath—all literary descendants of Wordsworth (for better or worse)—is that "what is presupposed is that their life and their situation is going to be eternally fascinating to you. And it isn't." Dickey adds in contrast, "I *am* interested in Roethke's relationship to the ocean, because that gets me *into* it. I can participate. I can't enter Lowell's family."[5] Wordsworth's writing puts him potentially in the same predicament that, according to Dickey, Lowell's writing does; however, he repeatedly finds a Roethkean solution—which is to write the self out of the natural world and one's imaginative relationship with it. Wordsworth understands that the adapting of one's life for a creative work must not be limited to an already existing biographical interest or be circumscribed by the author's vanity. It has to have a more universal relevance. One life must speak to other lives.

I want to conclude this book by explaining my occasional references to Dickey, who provides the epigraph for this book and who, I am proud to say, was my teacher—even if it was only for a semester. He died shortly after the course ended. Dickey convinced me that a great poet such as Wordsworth could actually exist in flesh, blood, and bone. Of course, I knew that Wordsworth existed—his remains are moldering in the churchyard of St. Oswald's Church at Grasmere. But I imagine that a man like Wordsworth must have been a man like Dickey. Obviously, I mean this in a figurative way because the hard-drinking Dickey could not have been more different in his various pursuits than the "simple water-drinking Bard" Wordsworth was in his.[6] But Dickey embodied for me the poetic spirit that I like to think also animated Wordsworth. The real-life Dickey that I knew was sometimes terrible in class—for whatever reason (you may have heard the stories)—but when he was on his game he was awe-inspiring and did seem to be "a favored being" in the way that Wordsworth claimed to be. And yet the bad days, his incoherent off-the-cuff lectures, his oh-this-again anecdotes about Burt Reynolds, and his surprising admiration of the movie *Halloween*, are just as memorable, just as valuable to me as his good days. And I am certain that a correspondent Wordsworthian breeze passed through me at his memorial service during a performance of "Dueling Banjos." Or did it? Does it matter whether it did or not? I choose to believe that it happened to me, and writing it just now made it happen. The more important question is: did my sense of this happening come from within or without?

In my copy of *The Complete Motion*, Dickey signed what probably was his usual autography—"For Daniel, in the Kingdom of the Imagination." But I choose to believe it was written just for me. I realize now that the mortification of the imagined immortal and then the creative re-integration of what remains as memory is fundamentally a Wordsworthian process of knowing, for Wordsworth is a poet of the non-event and un-epiphany, of the nearly significant and the not-quite-understood; he is, in other words, the poet of the mundane sublime. His is a poetry that anticipates disappointment in actually viewing the imagined summit, a poetry that crosses the Alps without knowing it and then gets lost while attempting to retrace its steps. But then, by accident, it finds the Simplon Pass, where all of the features of Nature

> [Are] all like workings of one mind, the features
> Of the same face, blossoms upon one tree,
> Characters of the great Apocalypse,
> The types and symbols of Eternity,
> Of first and last, and midst, and without end.[7]

Wordsworth can protest as much he likes that this happened when he and his friend Robert Jones walked down the Gondo ravine, but he, you, I, we all know that this amazing revelation happened when he wrote it. We know because we know what it feels like to write something so good that it seems to transcend our abilities. The sublime does occur in Wordsworth but it happens — if it can be said to happen — inside, where it has always been ready to happen. And the "one mind" that imparts itself to Wordsworth also can be said to include the minds of Wordsworth, Milton, to whom he here directly alludes, Dickey, all poets, and all of us who read and write ourselves.

Wordsworth's writing about himself, about daffodils or receiving the visiting of "one mighty Mind" atop Mount Snowdon is no more determinate for readers than is, say, Bruce Springsteen's writing about classic Chevrolets or prowling the boardwalks of the Jersey shore. We need not know those things or have had those experiences. What the maker seeks to do is to find figures from his life that will correspond with similarly peculiar ones from his readers' lives and then model for his readers what they can do with those figures, to produce creative fruits of their own and to repair imaginations that become impaired during the intercourse of everyday life.

Everyone can relate to the conclusion of Springsteen's "Thunder Road," where he sings ruefully but also hopefully, "it's a town full of losers and I'm pulling out of here to win." I suspect these lines resound more powerfully, with greater amplification, in the ears of dreamers, writers, and would-be rock-n-rollers coming of age in shithole towns all across America. Growing up in Roanoke, Virginia, I heard that call and started a band. I still hear its echo in the songs I write, record, and perform. But I think it resonates universally, too.

Wordsworth's song is not so different, and he sings it to other dreamers, writers, and would-be poets who have the ambition of being heroes in their own autobiographical epics. Or, as he writes in "Michael," he tells this particular story "for the sake / Of youthful Poets, who among these Hills / Will be my second Self when I am gone." He imparts the tradition to his successors and, as his predecessors did, achieves immortality. It is very rock-n-roll, isn't it? "It's better to burn out than to fade away," Neil Young sings. Those words are recapitulated, sadly without irony, in Kurt Cobain's suicide note. Unlike the young Romantics who died young, Wordsworth lived on and on. Some readers prefer to imagine that Wordsworth did burn out around the time of finishing the thirteen-book *Prelude* in 1805, rather than to face the master narrative of Wordsworth's long, slow decline. Maybe, in a weird way, on some subconscious level, that's another reason Wordsworth preserved himself young, as someone just about to be Wordsworth in *The Prelude*. That young Wordsworth is always becoming and is always alive, the "myself" aware of "two consciousnesses" eventually becomes "some other being," too. And so on. I see Dickey as a gloriously ferocious "second self" to Wordsworth— especially at the end of "For the Last Wolverine," which is a poem partly about extinction, but mostly about poetry, when he writes, "*Lord, let me die but not die / Out.*"[8]

Acknowledgments

I absolutely must thank Robert D. Richardson for seeing the potential in my project for the Muse Books series. Writing this book has been the most enjoyable project of my career, and I am deeply grateful to Professor Richardson for giving me this opportunity. Special thanks go also to Elisabeth Chretien, my editor at the University of Iowa Press, for her initial interest and for abundant encouragement, advice, and assistance throughout the process. For their love and support, I am grateful to my family, Wendy Warren and Sarah Margaret Robinson; and I am grateful to my band, Mark Graybill and Bob Falgie, mostly for the rocking. With many thanks, I want to acknowledge the support of this project provided by Dean Matthew Poslusny and Provost Stephen C. Wilhite at Widener University. I also owe a debt of personal gratitude to Grant Strine. Special thanks are due to Janine Utell for her brilliant insights and suggestions, to Jason Goldsmith for his amazing artwork, and to Susan Logsdon for her careful eye in the reading of proofs.

Because my thinking about Wordsworth has been influenced by a long and distinguished tradition of scholarship, I can only acknowledge my debts to those works that pertain most directly to this book by recommending them for further reading: David Bromwich, *Disowned by Memory; Wordsworth's Poetry of the 1790s* (University of Chicago Press, 1998); Paul de Man, "Autobiography as Defacement," *MLN* 94 (1979), 919–30; Paul H. Fry, *Wordsworth and the Poetry of What We Are* (Yale University Press, 2008); Stephen Gill, *William Wordsworth: A Life* (Oxford University Press, 1989); Richard Gravil, *Wordsworth's Bardic Vocation, 1787–1842* (Palgrave Macmillan, 2003); Geoffrey H. Hartman, *Wordsworth's Poetry, 1787–1814* (Yale University Press, 1964); Kenneth R. Johnston, *Wordsworth and The Re-*

cluse (Yale University Press, 1984); Nicholas Roe, *Wordsworth and Coleridge: The Radical Years* (Oxford University Press, 1988); Susan J. Wolfson, *The Questioning Presence: Wordsworth, Keats, and the Interrogative Mode in Romantic Poetry* (Cornell University Press, 1986); and Duncan Wu, *Wordsworth: An Inner Life* (Blackwell, 2002). To readers seeking an accessible overview of the lives of and the relationship between Wordsworth and Coleridge, I recommend Adam Sisman's *The Friendship: Wordsworth and Coleridge* (Viking, 2006).

The epigraph from "The Other," from *The Whole Motion*, © 1992 by James Dickey, reprinted by permission of Wesleyan University Press.

The epigraph from "Turning Back," from *The Boatloads*, © 2008 by Dan Albergotti, reprinted by permission of BOA Editions.

Notes

EPIGRAPHS

James Dickey, from "The Other," *The Complete Poetry of James Dickey*, ed. Ward Briggs (University of South Carolina Press, 2013), 75.

Dan Albergotti, from "Turning Back," *The Boatloads* (BOA Editions, 2008), 33.

PRELUDE

1 "Resolution and Independence," lines 48–49 (232).

2 To Sir George Beaumont, May 1, 1805. *The Letters of William and Dorothy Wordsworth: The Early Years*, 2nd edition, ed. Ernest de Selincourt and Chester L. Shaver (Oxford University Press, 1967), 586. Hereafter abbreviated as *Letters: Early Years*.

3 *The Prelude*, Book One, line 669 (318).

4 Blank verse is unrhymed iambic pentameter. Because of the many metrically irregular lines in his blank verse poems, Wordsworth occasionally was accused of writing prose that he set as ten-syllable lines in order to look like iambic pentameter. By varying the expectation of alternating stressed and unstressed syllables for a less rigid, more conversational effect, Wordsworth was following an example set by Coleridge who in turn was inspired by William Cowper.

5 *The Complete Poetry and Prose of William Blake*, ed. David V. Erdman (Anchor, 1988), 666.

6 *The Prelude*, Book One, lines 655–57 (318).

7 Preface to *Lyrical Ballads* (59, 60, 65–66, 73).

8 Blake, *Complete Poetry and Prose*, ed. Erdman, 665.

9 Jeffrey, from the *Edinburgh Review*, November 1814, *William Wordsworth: The Critical Heritage*, ed. Robert Woof (Routledge, 2001), 382.

10 *Letters of John Keats*, ed. Robert Gittings (Oxford University Press, 1990), 48.

11 Byron, from *Don Juan*, *Lord Byron: The Major Works*, ed. Jerome J. McGann (Oxford University Press, 2000), 514.

12 William Hazlitt, from "Mr Wordsworth," *The Selected Writings of William Hazlitt*, vol. 7, ed. Duncan Wu (Pickering & Chatto, 1998), 167.

13 *The Prelude*, Book Six, line 542 (390).

TWO CONSCIOUSNESSES

1 *The Prelude*, Book Two, lines 27–33 (319). These lines were drafted for the two-part Prelude and remain unchanged: see *The Prelude, 1798–1799*, ed. Stephen Parrish (Cornell University Press, 1977), 55.

2 *Letters of John Keats*, ed. Gittings, 61.

3 Wordsworth to Sir George Beaumont, February 1808, *The Letters of William and Dorothy Wordsworth: The Middle Years*, 2nd edition, Part 1, ed. Ernest de Selincourt and Mary Moorman (Oxford University Press, 1969–70), 195.

4 *Ibid.*, lines 76–77 (51).

5 *Ibid.*, lines 85–86 (51).

6 *Ibid.*, lines 89, 92, 96 (51).

7 *Ibid.*, line 112 (52).

8 *Ibid.*, lines 106–108 (51–52).

9 Blake, *Complete Poetry and Prose*, ed. Erdman, 702.

10 "Tintern Abbey," lines 42, 46–50 (50).

11 *Ibid.*, lines 23–24 (49).

12 "I wandered lonely as a Cloud," lines 14–15 (266).

13 *Ibid.*, lines 17–18 (266).

14 Fragment, *Lyrical Ballads, and Other Poems, 1797–1800*, ed. James Butler and Karen Green (Cornell University Press, 1992), 309.

15 *The Prelude, 1798–1799*, ed. Stephen Parrish (Cornell University Press, 1977), 115.

16 "Tintern Abbey," lines 109–112 (52).

17 James Dickey, *Sorties* (Louisiana State University Press, 1984), 164.

18 Preface to *Lyrical Ballads* (68).

19 *The Prelude, 1798–1799*, ed. Stephen Parrish (Cornell University Press, 1977), 54.

20 I here allude to Springsteen, Dickey, Woolf, and Blake. Wordsworth's experience atop Mount Snowdon in Wales is the climax of the thirteen-book and fourteen-book versions of *The Prelude*.

21 *Journals and Miscellaneous Notebooks of Ralph Waldo Emerson*, volume 15, ed. Susan Sutton Smith and Harrison Hayford (Harvard University Press, 1978), 99. Wordsworth, from "Ode," line 9 (281).

22 "Ode," line 18 (281).

23 *Ibid.*, lines 206, 132–33 (286, 284).

THE HISTORY OF A POET'S MIND

1 *The Prelude*, Book Thirteen, lines 404–10 (515).

2 To Anne Taylor, April 9, 1801, *Letters: Early Years*, 327.

3 Translation by R. S. Pine-Coffin, from the opening of Book XI of the *Confessions* (Penguin, 1961), 253.

4 Coleridge to Joseph Cottle, March 7, 1798, *Collected Letters of Samuel Taylor Coleridge*, ed. Earl Leslie Griggs (Clarendon Press, 1956), volume 1, 391. Abbreviated hereafter as *Collected Letters of Coleridge*.

5 Coleridge to John Thelwall, May 13, 1796, *Collected Letters of Coleridge*, vol. 1, 215.

6 Wordsworth to James Webbe Tobin, March 6, 1798, *Letters: Early Years*, 212.

7 Coleridge to Wordsworth, October 12, 1799, *Collected Letters of Coleridge*, volume 1, 538.

8 Wordsworth to Thomas Poole, April 9, 1801, *Letters: Early Years*, 324.

9 Wordsworth to Coleridge, March 6, 1804, *Letters: Early Years*, 452.

10 Coleridge to Richard Sharp, January 15, 1804, *Collected Letters of Coleridge*, volume 2, 1034.

11 *Biographia Literaria; Biographical Sketches of My Literary Life and Opinions*, two volumes ed. James Engell and W. Jackson Bate (Princeton UP, 1983), volume 2, 155–56.

12 Preface, *The Excursion*, ed. Sally Bushell, James A. Butler, and Michael C. Jaye (Cornell University Press, 2007), 38.

13 *The Prelude, 1798–1799*, ed. Parrish, 54.

14 From "Home at Grasmere," lines 249, 253–56. This poem was not published during Wordsworth's lifetime but evidently was intended to be part of "The Recluse."

15 Christopher Wordsworth, *Memoirs of William Wordsworth, Poet-Laureate, D.C.L.* two volumes (Moxon, 1851), volume 1, 313.

16 Preface, *The Excursion*, ed. Bushell, et al., 38.

17 In the United Kingdom, *The Trip*, directed by Michael Winterbottom, aired as a six-episode miniseries on the BBC.

18 Jonathan Bate, from his review of Reed's edition of *The Thirteen-Book Prelude*, *Modern Language Review*, vol. 89 (1994): 459–61, 460.

TRANCES OF THOUGHT

1 *The Prelude*, Book One, lines 20–25 (302).

2 *Ibid.*, Book Ten, lines 933–35 (481).

3 Wordsworth obliquely records his first meeting with Caroline in the sonnet beginning "It is a beauteous Evening, calm and free" (238).

4 "Tintern Abbey," lines 71–73 (51).

5 Wordsworth to Coleridge, December 1798, *Letters: Early Years*, 236. This letter includes some fragments that would later appear in *The Prelude.*

6 *The Prelude*, Book One, lines 6–8 (302).

7 *The Fourteen-Book Prelude*, ed. W. J. B. Owen (Cornell University Press, 1985), lines 6–8 (27).

8 *The Prelude*, Book Three, line 82 (333).

9 *The Prelude, 1798–1799*, ed. Parrish, 117. Parrish's edition includes photographs and transcriptions of the pages from the Goslar notebook, which is identified as MS. JJ, that pertain to the two-part *Prelude*.

10 *Ibid.*

11 *Ibid.*

12 *Ibid.*

13 *Ibid.*, 115.

14 *The Prelude*, Book One, 266–71 (308). See also *The Fourteen-Book Prelude*, ed. Owen, lines 263–69 (35); the lines in the fourteen-book version are unchanged. "Wicked and slothful" is from Matthew 25:26 (King James Version).

15 "'Was It for This . . . ?': Wordsworth's Virgilian Questionings," *Texas Studies in Literature and Language*, volume 33 (1991), 125–36, 130.

16 *Translations of Chaucer and Virgil*, ed. Bruce E. Graver (Cornell University Press, 1998), lines 780–81 (238).

17 *The Prelude*, Book One, lines 1, 42–43 (302, 303); *The Fourteen-Book Prelude*, ed. Owen, line 35 (28).

18 *The Prelude*, Book Seven, lines 4–5 (394).

19 Abrams, "The Correspondent Breeze: A Romantic Metaphor," *English Romantic Poets: Modern Essays in Criticism*, ed. M. H. Abrams (Oxford University Press, 1975), 37.

20 *The Prelude*, Book One, lines 41–47 (303).

21 *The Prelude, 1798–1799*, ed. Parrish, 117.

22 *The Prelude*, Book One, lines 50–54 (303).

A CHOSEN SON

1 "The Ruined Cottage," lines 76–79 (151).

2 *Paradise Lost*, Book Nine, lines 13–14. [Line numbers are the same in all editions of *Paradise Lost*]

3 *The Prelude*, Book One, lines 85–87 (304).

4 *Ibid.*, lines 124–41 (305).

5 *Ibid.*, lines 157–68 (306).

6 This five-book *Prelude* does not exist in any discrete state because Wordsworth immediately set upon revising and expanding it.

7 *The Prelude*, Book One, lines 180, 213–19 (306, 307). Milton recaps his rejected epic themes — the "Romantic" tales (that is, medieval chivalric romances), which Wordsworth mentions — in Book Nine of *Paradise Lost* (lines 25–41).

8 *Ibid.*, lines 230–31 (307).

9 *Ibid.*, lines 240–41 (308).

10 *Ibid.*, 668–74 (318).

11 "The Ruined Cottage," lines 76–85 (151).

12 *The Prelude, 1798–1799*, ed. Parrish, 159.

13 *Ibid.*

14 *Ibid.*, 65.

15 *The Prelude*, Book Three, line 556 (345).

16 *Ibid.*, lines 79–89 (333).

17 *Ibid.*, Book Four, lines 340–45 (356); Johnston, *Wordsworth and The Recluse* (Yale University Press, 1984), 137.

18 *The Prelude*, Book Six, lines 16, 32–33 (377).

19 *Ibid.*, 67–69 (378).

20 *The Prelude, 1798–1799*, ed. Parrish, 83. See also lines 68–73 (44–45).

21 *Ibid.*

22 *Ibid.*, lines 67–68 (44).

23 *Ibid.*, line 79–80 (45).

24 *The Prelude*, Book One, lines 351–55 (310).

25 *Ibid.*, lines 305–306 (309).

26 *Ibid.*, lines 418–20, 425–27, 436, 441 (312–13).

27 Wordsworth to Sir George Beaumont, June 3, 1805, *Letters: Early Years*, 594.

28 Preface, *The Excursion*, ed. Bushell, et al., 38.

29 Wordsworth to Richard Sharp, April 29, 1804, *Letters: Early Years*, 470.

30 Wordsworth to Thomas De Quincey, *Letters: Early Years*, 454.

31 *The Prelude*, Book Three, line 171 (335).

32 *Ibid.*, Book Four, lines 247–68 (354).

33 *Ibid.*, Book One, line 54 (303).

34 *Ibid.*, Book Three, lines 171–72, 177, 182, 188, 189, 191–92 (335–36).

35 *Ibid.*, lines 196–97, 199–201 (336).

36 *Ibid.*, Book One, line 15; *Paradise Lost*, Book Twelve, 646.

37 Coleridge to Lady Beaumont, April 3, 1815, *Collected Letters of Coleridge*, vol. 4, 564.

38 Coleridge to Wordsworth, May 30, 1815, *Collected Letters of Coleridge,* vol. 4, 574.

39 Coleridge to Lady Beaumont, March 26, 1804, *Collected Letters of Coleridge,* vol. 2, 1104.

40 Coleridge, "To William Wordsworth," lines 1 and 108, (manuscript version sent to Wordsworth) *The Prelude: 1799, 1805, 1850,* ed. Jonathan Wordsworth, M. H. Abrams, and Stephen Gill (Norton, 1979), 542–45.

41 *Ibid.,* lines 116, 119.

THERE WAS A BOY

1 "There was a Boy," *Lyrical Ballads, and Other Poems, 1797–1800,* ed. Butler and Green, lines 1–11 (139–40).

2 Coleridge to Wordsworth, December 10, 1798, *Collected Letters of Coleridge,* volume 1, 453.

3 *The Prelude, 1798–1799,* ed. Parrish, 87.

4 *Ibid.*

5 "The Pedlar" (Manuscript E), *The Ruined Cottage and The Pedlar,* ed. James Butler (Cornell University Press, 1979), lines 202–204 (398).

6 "There was a Boy," *Lyrical Ballads, and Other Poems, 1797–1800,* ed. Butler and Green, lines 21–22 (140).

7 *Ibid.,* lines 29–32 (141).

8 *The Fenwick Notes of William Wordsworth,* ed. Jared Curtis (Humanities-Ebooks, 2007), 60.

9 The boy of Winander passage appears in Book Five of *The Prelude,* lines 389–422 (370–71).

10 *The Prelude,* Book Two, lines 237–80 (325–26).

11 *The Prelude,* Book Two, lines 279–80 (326).

12 See the dialogue between the adult and the child in Wordsworth's "We Are Seven," which Dickens greatly admired, but be wary of assuming the adult narrator of the poem to represent Wordsworth's position (21–23).

13 "Ode," line 110 (283).

14 "My heart leaps up when I behold," line 7 (264).

15 "Ode," lines 144–48 (284).

16 *The Prelude,* Book Five, 532–36 (374).

17 "Ode," lines 62–65 (282).

18 *Fenwick Notes,* 161.

19 "Ode," lines 130–31, 59, 66–67, 75–76 (284, 282).

20 Preface to *Poems* (613).

SHRINES SO FRAIL

1 *The Prelude*, Book Five, lines 44–48 (361–62).

2 Coleridge to James Webbe Tobin, September 17, 1800, *Collected Letters of Coleridge*, vol. 1, 623.

3 Coleridge to Joseph Cottle, May 28, 1798, *Collected Letters of Coleridge*, vol. 1, 412.

4 "Advertisement," *Lyrical Ballads, and Other Poems, 1797–1800*, ed. Butler and Green, 739; Preface to *Lyrical Ballads*, 57–82.

5 "Elegy written in the same place upon the same occasion," lines 55–56; "Dirge," lines 41–42; *Lyrical Ballads, and Other Poems, 1797–1800*, ed. Butler and Green (300, 302).

6 "The Two April Mornings," lines 21–24, 53–56, 57–60 (114–15). See also "The Fountain" (115–17).

7 Coleridge to Thomas Poole, April 6, 1799, *Collected Letters of Coleridge*, vol. 1, 479.

8 "A Slumber Did My Spirit Seal," 103.

9 Wordsworth to James Webbe Tobin, March 6, 1798, *Letters: Early Years*, 211.

10 Wordsworth to Joseph Cottle, July 27, 1799, *Letters: Early Years*, 267.

11 Dorothy Wordsworth to Jane Marshall, May 11, 1808, *The Letters of William and Dorothy Wordsworth: The Middle Years*, 2nd edition, Part 1, ed. de Selincourt and Moorman, 236.

12 Wu, *Wordsworth: An Inner Life* (Blackwell, 2002), 216; *The Prelude*, Book Eight, line 727 (431).

13 *The Prelude*, Book Five, lines 37–48 (361–62).

14 *Ibid.*, 610–29 (376).

15 See Percy Bysshe Shelley's sonnet "To Wordsworth."

16 "Tintern Abbey," lines 140–41 (52).

17 "The Old Cumberland Beggar," line 146 (124).

18 *The Prelude*, Book Six, lines 630–31 (376).

19 *Ibid.*, lines 633–37 (376).

20 *The Thirteen-Book Prelude*, ed. Mark L. Reed (Cornell University Press, 1991), volume 1, 1276.

21 Preface, *The Excursion*, ed. Bushell, et al., 38.

22 *The Five-Book Prelude*, ed. Duncan Wu (Blackwell, 1997); *The Prelude: The Four Texts (1798, 1799, 1805, 1850)*, ed. Jonathan Wordsworth (Penguin, 1996).

SPOTS OF TIME

1 *The Prelude, 1798–1799,* ed. Parrish, lines 288–96 (50). Compare with *The Prelude,* Book Eleven, lines 258–79 (491).

2 G. E. Bentley, Jr., *Blake Records* (Oxford University Press, 1969), 312.

3 *The Prelude,* Book Eleven, lines 269–71 (491).

4 "Nutting," line 54 (119) (author's emphasis).

5 *The Prelude,* Book Eleven, lines 251–57 (490–91).

6 Book IX, lines 443–49, 513–118, *The Excursion,* ed. Bushell, et al., 287, 289–90.

7 Coleridge to Thomas Poole, March 23, 1801, *Collected Letters of Coleridge,* volume 2, 709.

8 *Biographia Literaria,* ed. Engell and Bate, volume 1, 304.

9 Preface to *Poems,* 607–15.

10 Wordsworth to John Wilson, June 7, 1802, *Letters: Early Years,* 355.

11 "Tintern Abbey," lines 106–108 (51–52).

12 *The Prelude,* Book Eleven, lines 260, 269–73 (491).

13 *The Prelude,* Book Twelve, line 32 (495).

14 *The Prelude,* Book Eleven, lines 177, 132–33, 185 (489, 487).

15 Mary Jacobus, *Romanticism, Writing and Sexual Difference: Essays on* The Prelude (Oxford University Press, 1989), 18.

16 *The Prelude,* Book Eleven, lines 309–11 (492).

17 *Ibid.,* lines 335–36, 342–43 (492–93).

18 Jacobus, *Romanticism, Writing and Sexual Difference,* 20.

19 Daniel Robinson, "*Elegiac Sonnets*: Charlotte Smith's Formal Paradoxy" *Papers on Language and Literature,* vol. 39 (2003), 185–220.

20 Preface to *Lyrical Ballads,* 74.

21 *The Prelude,* Book Six, lines 453–56 (388).

22 *Ibid.,* lines 456–61 (388).

23 *Ibid.,* line 466 (388).

24 Hartman, *Wordsworth's Poetry, 1787–1814* (Yale University Press, 1964), 41.

25 *The Prelude,* Book Six, lines 531–42 (390).

26 *The Prelude,* Book Thirteen, lines 42–43 (506).

27 *Ibid.,* lines 71–73 (506–507).

28 *The Fourteen-Book Prelude,* ed. W. J. B. Owen (Cornell University Press, 1985), lines 70–71 (259).

29 *The Prelude,* Book Thirteen, lines 239–40 (511).

30 *Ibid.,* line 170 (509).

31 *Ibid.,* lines 186, 192–93 (509–10).

32 *Ibid.,* lines 439, 442, 446–52 (516).

FINALE

1   "Michael, A Pastoral Poem," lines 34–39 (135).

2   Wordsworth to Lady Beaumont, May 21, 1807, *The Letters of William and Dorothy Wordsworth: The Middle Years*, 2nd edition, Part 1, ed. de Selincourt and Moorman, 146.

3   *Letters of John Keats*, ed. Gittings, 157.

4   Eric G. Wilson, *My Business Is To Create: Blake's Infinite Writing* (University of Iowa Press, 2011), 10.

5   Dickey, "The Art of Poetry No. 20," *The Paris Review*, no. 65 (Spring 1976). Available online at www.theparisreview.org/interviews.

6   Wordsworth, *Benjamin the Waggoner*, ed. Paul F. Betz (Cornell University Press, 1981), line 60 (48).

7   *The Prelude*, Book Six, lines 568–72 (391).

8   *Complete Poems of James Dickey*, ed. Briggs, 368.

index